Negotiating a
Complex World

NEW MILLENNIUM BOOKS
IN INTERNATIONAL STUDIES

Deborah J. Gerner, Series Editor

NEW MILLENNIUM BOOKS issue out of the unique position of the global system at the end of the cold war, the end of the twentieth century, and the beginning of a new millennium in which our understandings about war, peace, identity, sovereignty, security, and sustainability—whether economic, environmental, or ethical—are likely to be challenged. In the new millennium of international relations, new theories, new actors, and new policies and processes are all bound to be engaged. Books in the series will be of three types: compact core texts, supplementary texts, and hypertexts.

Editorial Board

Titles in the Series

Military–Civilian Interactions: Intervening in Humanitarian Crises
Thomas G. Weiss

Negotiating a Complex World: An Introduction to International Negotiation
Brigid Starkey, Mark A. Boyer, and Jonathan Wilkenfeld

Negotiating a Complex World

An Introduction to International Negotiation

Brigid Starkey, Mark A. Boyer,
and Jonathan Wilkenfeld

ROWMAN & LITTLEFIELD PUBLISHERS, INC.
Lanham • Boulder • New York • Oxford

ROWMAN & LITTLEFIELD PUBLISHERS, INC.

Published in the United States of America
by Rowman & Littlefield Publishers, Inc.
4720 Boston Way, Lanham, Maryland 20706

12 Hid's Copse Road
Cumnor Hill, Oxford OX2 9JJ, England

British Cataloguing in Publication Information Available

Library of Congress Cataloging-in-Publication Data
Starkey, Brigid, 1962–
    Negotiating a complex world : an introduction to international
negotiation / Brigid Starkey, Mark A. Boyer, and Jonathan
Wilkenfeld.
        p.   cm. — (New millennium books in international studies)
    Includes bibliographical references and index.
    alk. paper)
    1. Diplomatic negotiations in international disputes. I. Boyer,
Mark A. II. Wilkenfeld, Jonathan. III. Title. IV. Series.
JZ6045.S73 1999
327.1'7—dc21   99-28471

ISBN 0-8476-9044-X (cloth: alk. paper)
ISBN 0-8476-9045-8 (pbk.: alk. paper)

Printed in the United States of America

∞™ The paper used in this publication meets the minimum requirements
of American National Standard for Information Sciences—Permanence of
Paper for Printed Library Materials, ANSI Z.39.48–1984.

Contents

Contents

Illustrations

Figures

Photos

Boxes

Preface

It is not accidental that the three of us have come together to author a book on international negotiation at this particular time. What unites us is our nearly two-decades-long association with the ICONS project and the negotiation simulations that the project has spawned over the years. Our timing is dictated by the fast pace of developments in the electronic delivery of curricula and our enhanced ability to conduct our business, even international negotiations, via electronic media. In some sense, the real world is catching up with ICONS, although this bold assertion requires some explanation.

In the early 1980s, the International Communication and Negotiation Simulations project (or ICONS, as it came to be called) developed an approach to the teaching of international studies and foreign languages based on the use of foreign policy simulations delivered over available computer networks. These active learning exercises, which as of 1999 have involved participants at almost 150 universities in thirty-five countries around the world, place students in the roles of national decision makers as they represent their countries in negotiations on such topics as trade, human rights, the environment, nuclear proliferation, and various regional conflict arenas. The increasing availability of Internet access has allowed ICONS to bring together in joint exercises students representing different cultural, linguistic, and ideological backgrounds through the exchange of messages and electronic real-time conferencing. The principles of negotiation remain pretty constant, as do the strategies, tactics, and approaches employed. ICONS and other pedagogical approaches involving computers and networks have allowed us both to involve larger numbers of our students in these joint exercises and, at the same time, to give our students a glimpse of the possibilities for virtual negotiation available through technology. Having waited long enough for someone else to write this book, we eventually decided to do it ourselves.

We do not want the reader to come away with the mistaken impression that this is solely an ICONS supplementary text, although *Negotiating a*

Complex World can certainly be used effectively as such (see Afterword on virtual diplomacy). Rather, this book attempts to reach a broad audience of students who have a need for a more in-depth understanding of how nations and other international actors go about achieving their objectives through the give-and-take of the negotiation process. The skillful practice of negotiation can sometimes mean the difference between peace and war, and is often the only viable alternative to devolving into violence as a means of dispute resolution. In addition, in this increasingly interdependent world, strategies based more on the goal of achieving mutual benefit, rather than strict individual gain, will ultimately serve us better; effective use of the negotiation process can help us get there. This book attempts to provide the reader with some of the tools necessary to achieve this lofty objective, while drawing the reader's attention to cases in which negotiation has been used more or less effectively in recent years.

Although the three of us are ultimately the ones who put fingers to keyboard in the writing of this book, and are ultimately solely responsible for its content, many others over the years have contributed to the shaping of our ideas on the teaching of negotiation and the use of simulation techniques. These include Richard Brecht, Judith Torney-Purta, David Crookall, Joyce Kaufman, Leopoldo Schapira, Sarit Kraus, Robert Noel, Barry Hughes, and Harold Guetzkow. Others, including Doreen Bass, Patty Landis, Mike Miller, Mary Caprioli, Kim Holley, and Rosamaria Morales, who served as simulation coordinators and technical support for Project ICONS over the years, did much to provide the environment in which the study of negotiation could flourish. Jennifer Knerr, political science editor at Rowman and Littlefield, believed enough in this project to provide encouragement and guidance throughout, and Deborah J. Gerner, New Millennium Books series editor for Rowman and Littlefield, along with her distinguished editorial board, has provided important substantive input along the way. ICONS simulation director Beth Blake and program assistant Tim Wedig offered valuable insight and extensive support for this book project at critical junctures; Birhan Sener provided research assistance at the initial stages of the project. Betsy Kielman, managing director of Project ICONS, has guided this undertaking almost since its inception and helped manage the difficult task of coordinating among three authors, ever respectful of differing styles and sometimes tortured use of the English language. We gratefully acknowledge grant support from the U.S. Department of Education's Fund for the Improvement of Postsecondary Education (FIPSE), particularly for its funding of negotiation-related teaching materials. Finally, our institutions, the University of Maryland and the University of Connecticut, have provided the intellectual environment (and of course some resources) to see this project through.

1

Introduction

The desire to resolve problems amicably pervades all arenas of social organization. It is the function of negotiation to provide a channel for peaceful dispute resolution. As a process, negotiation involves common and often overlapping interests. It is, after all, the recognition of a mutual interest or joint problem that produces a dialogue. The underlying mutuality of the decision to negotiate is in fact the key to the process. However, negotiation discourses can also be highly conflictual. In the international realm, this means that negotiation is often all that stands between peace and war.

Negotiating a Complex World focuses on negotiation in the international diplomatic arena. In doing so, the book draws from the impressive body of academic literature on negotiation; hence, it is useful to begin with an overview of this hybrid topic. Owing to its relevance to so many different fields—including business, communication, law, political science, psychology, and conflict resolution—the academic literature on negotiation is broad and varied. Most books and articles on negotiation fall into one of four categories, as illustrated in figure 1.1. The horizontal axis plots the level of abstraction: at one end are the theoretical materials, which analyze the process of negotiation; at the other are the applied materials that provide hands-on tips on how to negotiate successfully. Along the vertical axis can be plotted the value orientation or approach of the negotiation process, ranging from those that are primarily competitive in approach to those that are primarily collaborative. This range is also categorized as integrative versus distributive. The easiest way to describe the opposing sides is according to the stark split on whether negotiations result in clear winners and losers or whether the only

Figure 1.1 Literature on Negotiation

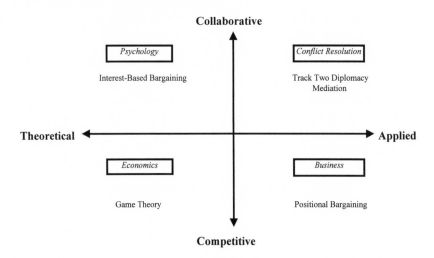

negotiated settlements that last are win-win ones (Murray 1986, 180–181). As an introduction to the study of international negotiation, *Negotiating a Complex World* draws concepts and examples from each of the categories described in figure 1.1. More specifically, the book provides a starting point for exploration of the many factors that impact the course of international negotiations and their outcomes, including an examination of the negotiation environment or setting, the issues and actors involved, and the strategies or moves that characterize the bargaining phase of these episodes.

Negotiation in Broad Context

There are many parallels to be drawn between the international negotiation process and the bargaining and tactics of negotiation in other forums. Newscasts report often about heated disagreements between labor and management at industrial plants, usually involving issues of pay, hours, benefits, job security, and worker productivity. Work stoppages, strikes, walkouts, and lockouts can be used as instruments in serious labor disputes to apply temporal and financial pressures on the disputants. The rough equivalents of such measures in the international context include such competitive diplomatic techniques as economic embargoes, diplomatic isolation, and political sanctions (George 1997). In the legal realm, figuring out who gets what in divorce proceedings—children, property, and often blame—can also involve bargaining at its most contentious. Indeed, over time, the comparison of such troubled pairs as the Israelis and the Palestinians or Northern Ireland's Catholics and Protestants to couples involved in hotly contested divorces represents a useful analogy:

all seek to split while arguing fiercely about the common property. Moreover, in the international arena, as in family disputes, third-party intervention, such as mediation or more binding arbitration, is sometimes the only way to bring parties to an agreement that will be fair and lasting.

A variety of popular negotiating tactics are also readily recognizable from one social setting to another. Acting as the "playground bully" is one such general tack, whereby ultimatums and threats are issued and the recipient is told exactly what will happen if there is a failure to comply—"My father will beat up your father." In the international system, this can translate into the threat "My state will invade yours." Another standard tactic is the offer–counteroffer approach, demonstrated in a car-lot transaction. Here, the salesperson normally starts off with an inflated figure for the car, so as to demonstrate flexibility when making the concession in price that the buyer will inevitably demand. An international parallel can be found in trade negotiations, when initial requests for market penetration, for example, are unreasonably high. Or consider the good cop–bad cop routine, whereby a suspect being questioned is led to believe that one of the interrogators is likely to become violent at any moment. The suspect is therefore urged to confess immediately to the nice cop before things get ugly. In recent years, the UN Security Council has often played the good cop, working out in front of the United States in such troubled regions as sub-Saharan Africa and the Balkans. The principles that underlie successful negotiations are also recognizable from one arena to another: power, trust, equity, and status.

Yet, while recognizing the very broad correspondences within varying negotiation environments, it is equally important to focus attention on the uniqueness of international negotiation. Diplomatic negotiation has particularly high stakes and tremendous visibility. Its connection to firmly established laws, standards, and practices can be much more tenuous than in these other forums. With recourse to enforcement and punishment mechanisms uncertain, the burden of responsibility on international negotiators to draft good, fair, solid agreements that all parties will respect is unmatched.

Negotiation in International Relations

Within the realm of international relations, diplomatic negotiation is central to the functioning of the system of nation-states that has evolved over time. As a process, it must be distinguished from other entities negotiating transnationally—a familiar endeavor for firms and other private companies operating in today's global economy. For example, the recent merger negotiations between American-based Chrysler and German-based Daimler-Benz took place outside of the inter-state arena; it did not involve governmental actors. In contrast, back in the late 1980s, Chrysler CEO Lee Iacocca traveled with American president George Bush on a trade mission to Japan. In this case, Chrysler was a contributing party to diplomatic negotiations between two nation-states.

Negotiating a Complex World is focused on international, diplomatic negotiation—broadly defined to take full account of new, nontraditional actors and issues that are changing the landscape of today's international system. It is, however, an international, rather than a transnational, focus that is most useful as an introduction to the subject. Despite proclamations and forecasts to the contrary, neither the nation-state nor the international system of states is dead as the new millennium dawns. What has changed are calculations of state interest and state navigation of the international system. Both have become much more complex, owing to the increased importance of such factors as economic globalization, international media, and subregionalism. These topics have become central to the study of international negotiation, both as the focus of many contemporary negotiation dialogues and, in some cases, as situational factors influencing those dialogues.

Traditional definitions of diplomatic negotiation stress official, state-to-state exchanges and tend to focus on the roles of important, individual players—presidents, prime ministers, foreign ministers, ambassadors, and generals. Indeed, more often than not, states and their leaders are still the central characters in international relations and in headline-grabbing negotiations. Nevertheless, with the proliferation of new states in the last fifty years, navigating the international system has become more difficult. Some of these states are extremely weak and cannot exercise their will in meaningful ways within their regions or in the larger international system. Almost all states must endure strong pulls on their central power from increasingly vocal ethnic and other identity groups, rival centers of power, and economic forces. Assumptions about uniform state motivations and responses to different situations—which are almost always oversimplified—are now more problematic than ever. The perception of the state as monolithic is being challenged. Moreover, calculations of national interest—long the guiding precept for foreign policy decisions—have been greatly complicated by a host of issues (environmental and resource concerns, for example) that now rival traditional military–security considerations in importance to various stakeholders in the state.

Tribal, clan, religious, and linguistic identifications are just some of the factors that complicate negotiation situations for state actors. They give political voice to nonstate actors of various kinds who increasingly figure into important diplomatic situations. Some argue that this is what went wrong with U.S.-led dealings with Lebanon in the 1980s and Somalia and Iraq in the 1990s, where insufficient attention was paid to internal social factors (Ferguson and Mansbach 1996, 33). Indeed, many of the most visible negotiation stories of the last several years have involved nonstate actors in crucial roles, including the pope, the Palestine Liberation Organization (PLO), the Irish Republican Army (IRA), and the Kosovo Liberation Army (KLA).

Looking closely at diplomatic negotiation entails the examination of some of the key processes in international relations as a whole. Negotiation highlights the extent to which foreign policy is not simply about the external relations of actors in the international system, but also about their internal political situations as well. Domestic constituencies are now better informed about international developments than ever before. Calculations of group interests other than those of the state figure more prominently into unfolding negotiation scenarios. American Jody Williams, for example, won the 1998 Nobel Peace Prize for her work on the International Campaign to Ban Landmines, even though the United States was loudly condemned during those same negotiations for its lax stance on the issue. Williams, an employee of Vietnam Veterans of America, worked on the campaign via electronic mail from her farm in Vermont. That work lasted for six years and involved representing the concerns of approximately 700 humanitarian and grassroots groups on the land mine issue.

Negotiation As a High-Stakes Game

There are many different ways to conceptualize the negotiation process, including through images of *stages, rounds,* and *phases.* This book offers the analogy of a board game to help organize the topic for the reader. This comparison of the international negotiation process to a game puts emphasis on the idea of strategic moves and countermoves. Key components of the process are presented as the board (the negotiation setting), the players (the negotiators), the stakes (the issues to be resolved), and the moves (the decisions the negotiators make). In fact, international negotiation can be viewed as the ultimate strategic contest. In cases of nuclear brinkmanship, such as the Cuban Missile Crisis of 1962, the highest possible stakes are at risk.

The game metaphor is admittedly a simple one, but it provides an entry point into a discussion of negotiation; a variety of contests can be examined in which players have different attributes and specific boards, stakes, and strategic moves available to them. A comparison of just three games— checkers, chess, and backgammon—highlights both the relationships to negotiation and the distinctions among them. Checkers is a game of attrition, suggesting a "hard negotiation" situation where the last one standing is the winner. There is only a single path to power, and that comes directly at the expense of the adversary. Difficult negotiations in protracted conflict situations, such as those between Ulster's Protestants and Catholics, offer a real-world equivalence. There is a sense that both sides are trying to outlast the other and finish first by simply keeping their own assets intact.

In chess, however, understanding one's opponent in a strategic sense is much more important. Each side has a wide variety of tools and options available to it, and the range of correct choices is determined by the choices of one's adversary. Knowledge of an opponent's history is an important strategic asset, as is an understanding of classic strategies of the game. The Americans and the Soviets during the cold war were often depicted as having been involved in a dangerous chess match.

Backgammon—in stark contrast to chess and checkers—introduces the element of luck to the strategy. Those who believe that fate plays an important role in negotiations favor this analogy. AbiNader (1998, C5) prefers this conception when he describes negotiating in the Middle East as a game of backgammon, or *tawla*, "in which dice and luck are significant factors in creating and closing opportunities for the opponent." This approach involves significant gambles, creating a more unpredictable negotiation process.

Winning may be defined differently in each of these games, although, as with all contests, outcomes are win-lose (zero-sum), with recognition of clear winners and losers. Negotiation in the real world is, of course, far more complicated. Collaborative approaches to negotiation are based on the assumption that it is possible to achieve win-win (non–zero-sum) outcomes, where the result is at least minimally acceptable to all involved. Moreover, real negotiation does not take place in a controlled environment, as is the case with board games. Situational factors—internal and external—have impacts on actual negotiations. The negotiation setting, for example, can be affected by a variety of factors, such as domestic elections, outbursts of conflict, misguided public statements, and economic and environmental crises.

Structuring Negotiation

This book explores the topic of international negotiation by illustrating how various contextual and situational factors influence the negotiation process. In the next section of this introductory chapter, two case examples are sketched out using the game metaphor and its main components: setting (the board), actors (players), issues (stakes), and strategy (moves). Subsequent chapters will look in more detail at each of these elements. Chapter 2 describes the way the international system setting interfaces with a number of situation-specific characteristics to influence negotiations. Chapter 3 surveys the various types of international actors in negotiations and examines motivational factors leading them to behave as they do in negotiation situations. Chapter 4 explores the different ways issues play out in negotiations and develops the notion of issue saliency to account for actor responses in various circumstances. Chapter 5 examines the "game" itself, where different strategic approaches help determine the outcome for all involved players.

The importance of each of these areas to an overall understanding of the negotiation process is illustrated through the two examples that follow. These provide brief sketches of how the negotiation game works in practice. These cases, the 1997 climate talks in Kyoto, Japan, and the 1997–1998 Iraqi weapons inspections crisis, demonstrate the interplay of contrasting characteristics within individual negotiation episodes. The use of examples to highlight key elements of the diplomatic negotiation process is a central feature of this text. Various tenets of the Kyoto climate talks case and the Iraqi weapons inspections crisis case will be referenced in subsequent chapters to help the reader place theoretical and conceptual points into a helpful context. In addition, there will be a number of other references to historical and contemporary examples, some of which will be more fully developed for the reader, including the Arab–Israeli (with emphasis on the Palestinian–Israeli relationship), Northern Ireland, and North American Free Trade Agreement (NAFTA) cases.

Kyoto represents a large, multilateral negotiation where nongovernmental actors played pivotal roles. The environmental issue of climate change is a tricky one for states, as it is traditionally not high on their list of priorities but central for some domestic or new "global" constituencies. As with the prior negotiations on global warming and its effects, these talks were set in a very constrained time frame. Delegations were given only ten days in which to negotiate a final agreement, the main points of which were to be drawn from preliminary negotiation rounds. The range of strategies on display in Japan ranged from the typical, such as stonewalling, to more sophisticated moves, such as the effort by the United States and other advanced industrial nations to shift the focus away from national accountability and implementation to joint or collective arrangements. Although rhetoric did run high at times, the overall tone of these negotiations was collaborative, as befits a public-goods dilemma such as that posed by global warming.

In contrast, the 1997–1998 U.S.–Iraqi standoff over the UN weapons inspections program involved, first of all, far fewer participants than did the negotiations in Kyoto. Washington, Baghdad, and the UN were the main parties to the resulting talks, although there were certainly many interested bystanders. UN secretary-general Kofi Annan's mediation mission in Baghdad was a clear case of crisis negotiations, occurring against a backdrop of likely military confrontation. Indeed, at the time of Annan's February 1998 trip to Baghdad, negotiation had almost been written off as a possible way to break the prolonged impasse between the United States and Iraq. Moreover, in contrast to the negotiations in Kyoto, this was a very traditional international negotiation situation: nation-states at loggerheads over issues of national security. A notable feature of this type of negotiation case is the key roles that individuals played. Annan's mediation role was highly specialized and crucial, given the probable consequences of a negotiation-channel collapse. Although individuals were also critical at strategic points in the Kyoto negotiations, personalities were not an important factor in that case.

Although the contrasts between the two cases are clear, there are also several noteworthy similarities. Both the negotiations in Kyoto and those in Baghdad exposed cracks in the Western alliance (plus Japan) of the post–World War II period in important areas of international policy. Moreover, in both Kyoto and Baghdad, U.S. credibility was very much in question. The Clinton administration was strongly criticized at home and abroad over the climate negotiations and in the lead-up to the Annan negotiations, where suggestions that the United States might be bullying Iraq were gaining prominence. There are other similarities, as well, in the areas of setting and strategy. Both cases illustrate the extent to which international negotiation has become a two-level game for political leaders, with significant domestic, as well as international, implications. In both cases, President Clinton had a very difficult time getting Congress to accept his negotiation positions. At the conclusion of each of these negotiation episodes, critics charged that the final agreements lacked vigor and were not workable in the long run because they were little more than face-saving devices for the participants.

Taking the Heat in Kyoto: The 1997 Climate Change Conference

Background

Many environmental problems are by nature transboundary in scope. This makes them classic public-goods issues, as a number of nation-states share concern over their fate yet must also share the burden of finding solutions to them. Pollution and overexploitation of resources are two major collective problems that have been magnified by intense population growth, urbanization, and industrialization during the twentieth century.

No problem has engendered as much controversy as what is popularly known as the global warming debate. Although scientists had long hypothesized that emissions of greenhouse gases—such as carbon dioxide, methane, nitrous oxide, and chlorofluorocarbons—negatively affect the environment by creating a "thick blanket" that traps heat in the atmosphere, it was not until 1990 that an official international report actually endorsed the theory. Established by the UN Environment Program and the World Meteorological Association, the Intergovernmental Panel on Climate Change (IPCC) released a report indicating that at least one group of scientists and technical experts had reached a consensus on the existence of a problem. The report asserted that emissions of greenhouse gases from such modern conveniences as automobiles, refrigerators, and air conditioners would cause rapid and harmful climate change if left unabated (Houghton, Jenkins and Ephraums 1990, 1). The panel projected that by the year 2100 the global temperature would rise between 1 and 3.5 degrees Celsius, with potentially profound effects on water levels, food availability, and species survival.

Not surprisingly, studies questioning these predictions were immediately forthcoming, notable among them Thomas Gale Moore's *Climate of Fear* (1998). But the 1985 discovery of the hole in the ozone layer over Antarctica had mobilized international public opinion on environmental concerns, and despite the uncertainty surrounding the issue, many seemed in favor of concerted international action. That action began at the 1992 Earth Summit in Rio de Janiero. There, working on a tight deadline, 152 states and the European Union (EU) signed the Framework

Convention on Climate Change. In it, they agreed that states would issue periodic reports on their national greenhouse gas emissions, share information about climate change strategies, and work toward the creation of cooperative strategies for funding and technology to combat climate change. They also agreed to accept a nonbinding commitment to take measures aimed at returning their greenhouse gas emissions to 1990 levels by the year 2000 (United Nations Framework Convention on Climate Change). It was this clause—which some thought much too ambitious and others deemed not nearly ambitious enough—that would ultimately cause the most difficulty for future rounds of climate negotiations.

The working group established to follow up the Rio meeting was the Conference of the Parties (COP), which held its first session—COP-1—in Berlin in 1995. The Berlin Mandate that came out of these meetings shocked many observers with its force. It stated that developed countries would have to do more than they had promised at Rio to reduce their greenhouse gas emissions: stabilization at 1990 levels would not be adequate (Anderson 1995, 7). The document was particularly noteworthy because it legitimized different treatment for developed and developing countries, a point for which many countries in the southern hemisphere had been arguing. The ensuing disagreement over whether the premise was fair continued on through COP-2 in Geneva in 1996 and into the Kyoto talks. The Berlin Mandate also gave rise to a battle of percentages among the developed countries, one that defined much of the negotiations in Kyoto.

Setup

In December 1997 the COP held its third session (COP-3) in Kyoto. The primary goal was for the parties to the 1992 UN Framework Convention on Climate Change to agree on a legal document—a binding protocol—that would specify national targets and timetables for cuts in greenhouse gas emissions. The meeting in Kyoto represented the climax of ten years of international climate negotiations. In this way it was not an independent event, but the continuation of a long process. Climate negotiations are arduous and, despite moments of high drama during the eleven-day Kyoto negotiations, generally highly technical talks that are not readily accessible to nonexperts. The ongoing quest for a meaningful climate treaty has spawned a large community of people whose involvement in the issue is a full-time endeavor. Although complex, these negotiations involve a single issue, and despite the pleas for urgency voiced by many environmentalists, the negotiations are distinctly noncrisis in nature for the governments involved. These were negotiations with a past, as well as a future.

This legacy factor was perhaps the defining characteristic of the Kyoto negotiations. Many participants and analysts had considered the Framework Convention on Climate Change that came out of the 1992 Rio Earth Summit to be deeply flawed. The main criticism was that it did not bind its signatories to any definite action. While some lauded the progress made in "only fifteen months" on the Rio convention, others pointed to this as the problem; such a difficult issue would take much longer to work through. They criticized the pressure that deadlines before and at Rio presented to participants. The agreement was denounced as hurried and weak, and critics repeated these criticisms about the Kyoto negotiations. It was widely argued that the ten-day deadline for Kyoto was too constraining. These talks would have to involve arduous negotiations, critics argued, because the leadup talks in Berlin (COP-1) and Geneva (COP-2), had failed to reach consensus on the so-called Berlin Mandate— the need for the industrialized countries to sign on to more stringent and binding emissions cuts than less-developed nations.

In addition to the legacy- and time-factor characteristics, the difficult nature of the core issue of climate change heavily influenced the Kyoto negotiations. Questions of scientific veracity, social relevance, and political expediency were the unspoken stimuli behind the negotiation positions taken in Japan. Strong international leadership from the United States, the leader in so many other arenas, was also noticeably absent. In fact, the U.S. delegation had trouble shedding the label of world's heaviest greenhouse gas polluter and major obstructionist in the talks. Movement on the issue was made more difficult in the lead-up to Kyoto by the resistance from the U.S. Congress, which had consistently questioned the need for any action, as well as the economic price that would be paid for it. Ecology interest groups were quick to point out that the purpose of the meeting for state participants seemed to be how to shift the blame and the burden onto others. The Americans kept a finger pointed at the big developing nations (India, Brazil, etc.) in Kyoto while trying to deflect the embarrassing scrutiny of the Europeans away from their own negotiation stance. The object at Kyoto, even a noncynical observer would probably have had to admit, seemed to be how to please the "green" constituencies at home while keeping one's national business and industrial interests out of regulation's way. This quest for loopholes led Greenpeace, the well-known transnational group, to declare at conference end: "[We] estimate that the agreement, when all loopholes are considered, will result in no real reductions from the 1990 levels" (Environmental News Network 1997). But even this pessimistic conclusion cannot take away from the high drama and theatrics of the eleven days—one over the deadline—in Kyoto.

The Players

The Kyoto conference hosted 2,200 official delegates from 159 nation-states. The key actors can be grouped into five clusters: the EU—the advanced industrial countries of western Europe; the non-EU, developed countries of Japan, the United States, Switzerland, Canada, Australia, Norway, and New Zealand; the "transitional economies"—the industrialized countries of central and eastern Europe and the former Soviet Union; the "Group of 77"—China, India, and over 130 other so-called developing countries; and the Alliance of Small Island States (AOSIS)—42 mainly Caribbean and Pacific island nations.

The intentions of the different groups varied tremendously along a continuum from "serious about negotiating" to "trying to stall." The undisputed leader of the latter group was the United States. Having criticized George Bush's proposal at Rio to stabilize U.S. carbon dioxide emissions by the year 2000, the Clinton–Gore administration had actually done much worse during its five years in office. With fuel consumption way up as a result of the booming economy and the popularity of large recreational vehicles, the White House's negotiation stance was to fulfill Bush's target, ten years later than originally promised (Mott 1997)! The United States called for stabilization of emissions at 1990 levels by 2008–2012. Although disguised by a lot of confusing numbers, the target that the Japanese proposed was basically the same—stabilization by the industrialized countries by 2012. The EU focused its targets on three of the six greenhouse gases, also using 1990 levels as the base, and called for a reduction of 7.5 percent by 2005 and 15 percent by 2010. The Group of 77 had goals close to those of the EU, but it is vital to note that these were goals they held for the industrialized countries only, not for themselves. They resisted the pressure of the United States and others to bring them into the agreement, arguing that as developing nations their economic growth and trade competitiveness would be harmed by adherence to an emissions reduction regime. The AOSIS put forward the most ambitious target by far—calling for the developed countries to agree to 20 percent reductions by 2005. In caucus sessions prior to the Kyoto summit, it had laid the groundwork for this target by articulating its deep concerns about increases in sea levels owing to climate change. Indeed, it argued, a rise in the earth's temperature could be devastating to its member islands.

The conference was also noteworthy for the high-profile presence of various nongovernmental actors, who tried to lobby conference participants and court international public opinion either for or against a protocol during the eleven days of negotiations. The interested parties included business and industrial groups from the energy, electric, chemical, iron and steel, and paper and timber sectors. With the exception of nuclear energy representatives, whose industry stood to gain from regulations on other energy providers, the others were against a climate treaty, which they argued would negatively impact jobs and economic growth in general. Also highly visible, but on the other side of the fence, were environmental groups lobbying hard for a meaningful protocol. Along with Greenpeace, there were hundreds of other grassroots organizations and associations at work in Kyoto, including the Japanese Kiko Forum—a coalition of more than 150 Japanese environmental nongovernmental organizations (NGOs) mobilized on the climate change issue; the German NGO Forum on Environment and Development; the Friends of the Earth–UK; and the Worldwide Fund for Nature. These groups were creative and energetic in the mediums they used to share information, analyze events, and attempt to sway the outcome of the Kyoto talks. European NGOs sponsored a "climate train" across Europe en route to the convention, and many groups used the Internet to broadcast news and analysis to Kyoto watchers around the world in the form of daily diaries and newsletters from the convention floor. The newsletter *ECO* gained particular notoriety among delegates for its lampooning of the slow progress and doublespeak that its authors felt were dominating the convention. Keen observers and analysts also came to Kyoto from various scientific and technical groups, such as the Union of Concerned Scientists. Together, all of these nongovernmental actors took on very high-profile roles in Kyoto as advisers to national delegations and also as independent entities.

At the individual level of analysis, only two players stood out at the Kyoto talks. These were COP-3 chairman Raul Estrada-Oyuela of Argentina, who brokered the final compromise agreement, and U.S. vice president Al Gore, whose "rescue mission" to Kyoto at the one-week mark of the conference made for humorous headlines, such as "Kyoto Gets Gored" (Smith and Sheehan 1997) and "Full Gore on Kyoto" (Media Reality Check 1997). Fingered by the media in Kyoto as the main obstructionist to negotiation progress, the Clinton administration hoped Gore could promote cooperation among the United States, Japan, and the EU, but Gore also directed international public attention to the talks and the importance of the topic at hand. His trip, his remarks, and his apparent blessing for U.S. acceptance of more substantial emissions cuts got the American delegation actually involved in bargaining and gave a much-needed boost to the process in Kyoto.

The Stakes

Costs and benefits to the parties involved are of major importance to the ultimate success or failure of negotiations. Environmental treaties are particularly tricky because the benefits are often very abstract, involving notions of making the planet safer for future generations, while the costs can involve such politically unpopular outcomes as plant closings, job losses, and new taxes. On a basic level, all states and societies have an interest in an issue such as global warming. Assuming that the dire predictions concerning its advent and consequences are true, there is a general interest in controlling greenhouse gas emissions, but obviously the issue is of greater importance to some states than to others. The microstates in the AOSIS, for example, feel that global warming threatens their very physical survival. For them, this environmental issue is a life-or-death matter, since these island nations could literally be underwater as a result of even modest increases in sea levels caused by melting polar ice caps.

Other states, classified by some scholars as "postindustrial"—Canada, western Europe, Japan, the United States—now treat many environmental problems as security issues as well. This higher place for ecological concerns on national political agendas can be attributed to interest group pressure in highly mobilized civil societies, where such quality-of-life issues are now the business of the state. They are not popular items for these governments, however, because they involve very painful trade-offs. Estimates circulating in U.S. small-business circles prior to the Kyoto conference, for example, suggested that the Clinton administration's proposal for a carbon dioxide tax would cost the American economy $350 billion a year in reduced production of goods and services (Kerrigan 1997). Still, given the increasing dedication of resources and attention, environmental issues seem here to stay on these countries' international agendas. For the majority of other states in the international system—newly industrialized or at various levels of development—the ecology of global warming is not high on their national political agendas. Their interests in the Kyoto negotiations were dominated by a relative-gains perspective—to get the industrialized states to commit to meaningful emissions cuts while keeping themselves out of any agreement. For these developing countries, it is imperative that the rich, northern countries take responsibility for the costs of development of the newly industrialized nations. This perspective reflects the persistent north–south divide that characterizes negotiations on many environmental and economic issues.

These states were relatively successful at keeping the spotlight off of themselves in Kyoto, more so than Japan and the United States, which attracted a great deal of the media and public attention. Japan was under scrutiny as the host of these talks—a role that many in the international arena feel it has too often shunned since its rise to international power. For the United States, its credibility in the environmental arena was at stake in Kyoto. Washington's performance in Rio was widely condemned as obstructionist and self-serving, while many in and outside the United States were waiting to see if Clinton and Gore would redeem American environmental credentials, as well as their own.

Big issues and important relationships were on trial in Kyoto. Environmentalists had to face the question of whether there could be concerted international action on a matter over which the scientific community had not yet reached consensus. At issue: could something like global warming ever be adequately proven before it actually happened? Other questions included the matter of who would lead in the development of international environmental policy—the EU, which has worked hard to build some credentials in this area, or the United States, which has not, but which has such power on the world political stage that it can automatically assert itself in any forum. Also at stake were nothing less than the prevailing definitions of "developing" and "transitional" in the international economic system. The economic classifications of Brazil, China, India, Mexico, and the post-communist European states were all contentious in the debate of who would have to do what in a climate treaty. The United States and other western states argued that such a treaty would not make sense if many big polluters were not party to it.

The Kyoto negotiations provide some classic examples of two-level games. At the same time that it is international in scope and worthy of a global summit, an environmental issue such as climate change also has an important domestic dimension. In the United States, Congress must ratify any treaty agreements the executive branch of government negotiates. In the case of the Kyoto negotiations, the U.S. Senate made its feelings clear prior to the summit when it voted 95–0 for the Byrd–Hagel resolution, a nonbinding document that spelled out the Senate's serious reservations about the UN-sponsored climate talks. However, the American negotiating team, led by Under-Secretary of State Stuart Eizenstat, also had to respond to the domestic environmental lobby, which was very high profile in Kyoto. The U.S. delegation could not afford simply to take an obstructionist position and stick to it. Two-level games were also being played out in Germany and Japan, among other countries, where highly mobilized domestic interest groups—pro–climate change treaty—were pressuring their respective countries via the media and public opinion to take proactive stances.

The Moves

The end goal of improved air quality represents a public good, the achievement of which requires a cooperative effort across national boundaries. Herein lies the strategic dilemma that environmental problems present for states in the international system: pollution does not recognize national boundaries. States are unable to solve ozone depletion or acid rain problems on their own, but cooperation among states is not easy to achieve. They are inherently suspicious of one another and rely on definitions of national interest that are derived from relative gains: if you won, I must have lost. More often than not, a "tragedy of the commons" scenario develops in relation to the collaborative, long-range planning needed to combat environmental problems. In this metaphor, originally suggested by biologist Garrett Hardin, each individual herder on a medieval commons (open grazing pasture) would act in apparent self-interest and maximize his or her use of the commons by introducing as many additional cattle as possible. The outcome was the ruin, through overgrazing, of the commons and the resultant starvation of the herds (Hardin 1968).

The analogy to states in the international system, of course, is that political leaders are usually unwilling to implement measures unpopular at home—pay the costs—for benefits that will come in the longer term and are dependent on similar decisions and actions on the part of other states. The need for collective action is stymied by the lack of trust among states.

Given this lack of trust, it is not surprising that positional bargaining dominated the Kyoto negotiations. This intransigence is captured in the competing percentage rates: the EU with its 15.5 percent versus Japan's 5 percent rate and Chairman Estrada's professed dream at the conclusion of the talks that the outcome be a 6 percent cut. Some delegations even seemed unsure of what their numbers stood for at times. The United States was pushing for stabilization of emissions at 1990 levels, which was generally perceived as a technique to achieve a zero percent solution. But in fact, for the United States to go back to 1990 levels in 2000 would necessitate a 13 percent reduction in emissions (Mott 1997, cited above)! The Japanese delegation, for its part, created confusion for others at one point on the issue of whether the base level in its proposal was 1990 or some other year.

But there were also some more sophisticated moves at the Kyoto talks. In addition to relying on a notion of stabilization in place of specific target cuts, the United States also pushed for more complex approaches to the issue of national responsibility. Among the concepts the American delegation advocated were differentiation—the sharing of a target by the developed countries, allowing them variable national rates as part of the overall effort to meet the target; flexibility, the ability of states to buy and sell unused emissions quota points; and joint implementation, the ability to receive national credit for emissions reductions financed in and for other countries (Anderson 1995). Critics of the U.S. position condemned these various tools as ploys developed explicitly to avoid national responsibility. For the Clinton administration, however, they represented ways to achieve congressional cooperation at the important domestic or second-level dimension of the negotiations.

The need for congressional approval was clearly behind the major U.S. effort in Kyoto to bring the developing countries into the agreement. Although responsible for two-thirds of past emissions and approximately 75 percent of current emissions, the United States and fellow Organization for Economic Cooperation and Development (OECD) countries have been increasingly focused on the future culpability of developing countries in the area of emissions (United Nations Environment Programme). Sensitive to political opinion at home, where the NAFTA negotiations had spurred controversy on the environmental responsibilities of Mexico and other industrialized developing states (Brazil, India, China), the U.S. delegation pushed hard on the need for those states to adhere to a climate regime.

As the deadline loomed in Kyoto, there were standoffs on these proposals for developing-country inclusion and the acceptability of protocol language that would allow states to seek and trade greenhouse gas credits. China and India were outspoken in their opposition to both ideas. The Chinese and American delegations were actually seen and heard "snarling" at one another about these provisions inside a conference room on the tenth day in Kyoto (Warrick 1997).

There was no doubt on that tenth day that the original deadline for the end of the talks was real—not simply an artificial negotiation device.

Upon hearing of a one-day conference extension, many delegates panicked as they rushed to make changes to their airline tickets. Negotiations were complicated at this last minute for the Russian and Chinese delegations, both of which lost their translators when the contracts governing their translation services expired at midnight on December 10.

In the end, COP-3 chairman Estrada crafted a compromise that had the United States accepting defeat on the provision of "meaningful participation by developing nations" in return for inclusion in the protocol of language on the acceptability of emissions trading and related ideas as subjects for further negotiation among the parties. Even this may not have been enough to force agreement were it not for a procedural rule that allowed Estrada to decide when consensus had been reached. This he did by quickly reading the compromise language and then declaring the debate over with a bang of his gavel. Thirty-eight industrialized countries signed the protocol agreement. The deal committed them to cuts in emissions of greenhouse gases averaging 5.2 percent from 1990 levels, to be achieved during the 2008–2012 period (BBC News 1997).

Exciting as this endgame was, it did not represent a conclusion to the climate negotiations. Indeed, the most difficult questions were once again pushed back for consideration at future meetings—COP-4 (1998), COP-5 (1999), and COP-6 (2000). As observed in the *Christian Science Monitor* at the end of the Kyoto talks, "the hard part is over . . . but now comes the hard part" (Barr and Goodrich 1997). Developments in Buenos Aires in 1998 reinforced the veracity of this prediction; progress on substantive issues gave way to agreement on timetables for realizing the goals laid down in Kyoto. Countries like the United States went ahead and signed the global warming treaty in Buenos Aires but without ratification from Congress. Much more than a formality, ratification by Congress may not ever take place. Criticism remains strong for a commitment to reduce emissions by approximately one-third by 2012. For a country that seems to have moved far away from energy conservation measures during the last decade, making good on this commitment will be no easy task.

The Kyoto protocol agreement does not really seem to represent a win for anyone involved. It is, rather, a classic compromise outcome, where no side lost too badly. The negotiators never reached the stage of collaborative problem solving. If they had done so, a postmortem piece in the influential journal *Foreign Affairs* argued, they would have moved toward framing the negotiation issue differently. Rather than national emissions *targets*, they would have tried to define mutually agreed-upon *actions*, "such as a nationally collected tax on greenhouse gas emissions"—something all signatories would agree to establish (Cooper 1998, 68). In the final analysis, the Kyoto Protocol to the Framework Convention on Climate Change may be viewed historically as an essential step in a long, arduous process. But if future climate negotiations end in failure, then it will likely be seen as nothing more than a face-saving agreement, a way around serious action on the greenhouse gas issue.

"UNSCOM Plus the Suits":
Kofi Annan's Mediation Mission to Baghdad

Background

One of the most persistent military–security conflicts to threaten world peace since the end of the cold war has been the standoff between the United States and Iraq. It offers a good example of an iterated or repeated negotiation situation and a case of hostile diplomacy where the pendulum has continuously swung for a nine-year period between harsh words and punitive action. The now prolonged conflict began in August 1990 with the decision by Iraqi leader Saddam Hussein to invade neighboring Kuwait. In need of money to finance recovery from the eight-year war with the Islamic Republic of Iran, Saddam Hussein was clearly testing for weaknesses in the ill-defined, post–cold war international order, hoping that George Bush's "new world order" would be one in which regional players would be allowed to fight it out on their own terms without superpower interference. In this, Saddam Hussein miscalculated badly, and his troops were ultimately soundly defeated by the American-led, thirty-seven–country coalition of forces in the Desert Storm and Desert Saber military operations.

However, criticisms that the Allied Coalition pulled out of Iraq in 1991 before the job was complete proved valid, as within months of the cease-fire agreement Saddam Hussein was provoking international action once again with his attacks on the Iraqi Kurdish and Shiite populations. Indeed, between the February 1991 cease-fire and the December 1998 Desert Fox air attacks on Baghdad by the United States and Britain, there were nine standoffs of varying magnitudes between Washington and Baghdad (*Washington Post* 1998). Collectively, these incidents can be grouped into three broad categories: (1) Iraqi invasion of Kuwait and aftermath, (2) post–cease-fire attacks on populations in Iraq, and (3) inspections crises.

This case study focuses on the inspections crises period of the conflict and specifically on the attempt by UN secretary-general Kofi Annan to mediate hostilities between the United States and Iraq in February 1998. In fact, Annan's mission represents one of the only true negotiation episodes in this protracted struggle. Many of the former coalition members urged his involvement during the winter of 1997, when it became apparent that Iraq and the United States were headed back to the brink of war after Iraq refused to allow a multinational team of inspectors from the UN Special Commission on Iraq (UNSCOM) to fulfill its mandate to inspect certain sites. Declaring some presidential and other "sovereign" sites to be sensitive and objecting to the perceived American dominance of the inspections process, Iraq continued to refuse to cooperate with several key provisions of the cease-fire from the 1991 war. This was made more serious by the fact that a top Iraqi military leader, upon his defection in 1995, had provided UNSCOM with documents on Iraq's continued weapons program.

When the Iraqis barred from entry two American inspectors and then expelled the remaining six in October and November 1997, tempers at UNSCOM and in Washington and Baghdad began to flare again. The Russians managed to defuse the crisis temporarily by suggesting that certain sites be off-limits to the inspectors for the time being, but by January of the new year, Iraq was once again complaining about the composition of the inspection teams. This time, it went so far as to expel American team member Scott Ritter, whom it accused of being a spy.

Setup

After the Ritter expulsion and when Iraq refused an American-led UNSCOM inspection team access to a sensitive site in early January 1998, actions and reactions from the two sides seemed predetermined. For Iraq, seven years of being under scrutiny was long enough. The question of whether it had satisfied international demands during that period was secondary to what it deemed to be an unacceptably long period of ostracism and punishment. In its last face-to-face meeting before the negotiations took on an overtly hostile tone, Iraqi deputy prime minister Tariq Aziz actually urged UNSCOM director Richard Butler to "just close the books on us and let's move on." (United Nations 1998). One could almost hear the cries of exasperation from the United States and the members of the commission. They felt that Iraq was continuing to deliberately hide progress on its weapons programs and was being tipped off from intelligence sources—probably Russian, they believed—about the times and locations of what were supposed to be surprise inspections. They believed they had shown patience and restraint with Iraq but that this approach had failed. Their call now was for immediate adherence to the terms of the 1991 cease-fire agreement, foremost of which was respect for the UNSCOM mandate. In fact, they looked past the diplomatic channel and began to prepare in earnest for military action. Given the history between these parties, what might have been dismissed as an elaborate American bluff in another situation was apparently taken at face value in this case.

Momentum toward a U.S. attack was halted, however, by an American Town Hall Meeting at Ohio State University on February 18, 1998. Having sent Secretary of State Madeleine Albright and Secretary of Defense William Cohen overseas to try to drum up support for the U.S. position, the Clinton administration decided to have one of its hallmark town meetings, ostensibly to show the world that Americans were behind their government. Instead, the nationally televised event had exactly the opposite effect. Six thousand self-selected citizens showed up in Columbus,

Ohio, and proceeded to put Albright, Cohen, and National Security Adviser Sandy Berger on notice that the government's case for U.S. military action in Iraq had not been articulated to their satisfaction. Albright was repeatedly shouted down in midsentence and looked baffled and disturbed as people asked such questions as "Why bomb Iraq when other countries have committed similar violations?" or "Why does the U.S. apply different standards of justice to these countries?" And "I don't understand how a military strike by the United States is going to ensure future compliance. I'm seeing a pattern here, and I don't see how one military strike is going to end it" (U.S. Department of State 1998).

Serious questions and reservations were being expressed at home and abroad. The Clinton administration had not succeeded in reviving the Allied Coalition that President Bush had assembled, and the hostility that many of its neighbors had shown Iraq during the 1991 Gulf War seemed to have changed. Now, the focus was more on the people of Iraq and what they had suffered since 1991. Disillusionment with the Palestinian–Israeli peace process was further aggravating Arab opinion against the idea of retargeting Iraq. The Bush administration had explicitly linked future security in the Persian Gulf to progress in the negotiations between the Palestinians and the Israelis when it instigated the Madrid Process at the end of the war. At the time, this grand gesture seemed part of an agreement with Arab leaders to address the Palestinian issue in the aftermath of the American intervention in the Gulf. This strategy was an attempt to undo the link Saddam Hussein had made between his invasion of Kuwait and the presence of Israel in the region. However, the continuing intractability of the Palestinian–Israeli issue was adding to the Clinton administration's troubles at a critical juncture for its Gulf policy. Taken aback by the reaction in Columbus, Ohio, and under fire for the then-breaking news about the Monica Lewinsky affair, the Clinton team gave renewed attention to alternatives to a military campaign.

The Players

The original Allied Coalition against Iraq, or the Coalition of Member States Cooperating with Kuwait, as it was formally termed, numbered thirty-seven. George Bush's crafting of this impressive alliance against Iraq in 1990 is widely viewed as the outstanding diplomatic achievement of his four-year presidency. However, when trouble erupted again in the Gulf during the winter of 1997, a good number of these states were noncommittal or even openly opposed to a renewal of military hostilities against Baghdad. While Britain, Canada, Germany, and Kuwait ultimately offered to support a U.S. air campaign, there were prominent dissenters on this course of action, including Egypt, China, France, Greece, Italy, the Netherlands, Pakistan, Spain, Russia, and Turkey, as well as the Gulf Cooperation Council (GCC) states of Bahrain, Oman, Qatar, Saudi Arabia, and the United Arab Emirates.

For many of these states, bombing Baghdad to punish noncompliance with the UN monitoring regime was not a suitable tool of persuasion. In fact, support for the notion of American air strikes in late 1997 was at first so low that it looked like the United States would be virtually going it alone. This led U.S. secretary of state Madeleine Albright to take to the road to try to win support for the American position. Her efforts were given a boost when Russian attempts to defuse the crisis were discredited after allegations surfaced regarding Russia's complicity in the building of Iraq's biological weapons arsenal. In early February 1998, well after the inspections crisis was in full swing, the news broke that UNSCOM had uncovered evidence of an illicit 1995 deal between Moscow and Baghdad, which had the latter paying for and receiving sophisticated fermentation equipment that could be used to develop biological weapons. Not only would this alleged deal have violated the UN-authorized embargo on sales of sensitive materials to Iraq, it also suggested duplicity in Russia's support of Iraq at the Security Council and its suspected tip-offs to the Iraqis concerning UNSCOM inspection plans. It might even account for President Yeltsin's alarming comment that a U.S. bombing of Iraq over the inspections issue could lead to "world war" (Smith 1998).

The discrediting of Russia as an honest broker in the crisis put the United States back in the driver's seat temporarily. Washington rebuffed French attempts to settle the crisis and began to prepare in earnest for military action. Cautious support for a mediation attempt by UN secretary general Kofi Annan was offered only when it became clear that American public opinion—let alone international opinion—continued to be ambivalent about the proposed U.S. bombing campaign.

With the coalition not coming together as it had in 1990, this diplomatic crisis had many high-profile individuals in key roles. Although the UN was heavily involved in an institutional sense through both UNSCOM and the Secretary-General's Office, it was actually the respective chiefs themselves who garnered the most attention—the outspoken Australian Richard Butler and the soft-spoken Ghanaian Kofi Annan. Their roles were for the most part separate—Butler trying to convey the Commission's concerns over Iraq's continued noncompliance with the monitoring regime and, therefore, in full support of the U.S. position; and Annan voicing support for a negotiated settlement to the escalating tensions and trying to maintain a sense of diplomatic fairness to all parties. But their paths did cross in early February when the Russian delegation at the UN complained loudly about Butler's assertion that Iraqi weapons posed a serious threat to Israel. This prompted Annan to demand that Butler cease giving interviews to the media. No doubt this action raised the secretary-general's stock with Saddam Hussein, who, somewhat surprisingly to many observers, welcomed Annan to Baghdad in his role as mediator.

The roles that American president Bill Clinton, his secretary of state Madeleine Albright, Iraqi president Saddam Hussein, and his deputy prime minister Tariq Aziz played were all fairly predictable during the course of the crisis. The two presidents rattled their sabers, contributing to an air of urgency while their top diplomats conducted a war of words through the international media and met with various of their counterparts to try to win support for their respective positions. The Iraqis, it can be said, seemed more media savvy than they had during the Gulf War of 1990–1991, and this time did not personalize their public relations effort around Saddam Hussein himself. Instead, they insisted that they were being wrongly accused of weapons violations and continued to argue that it was only fair that the seven-year-old economic sanctions against them be lifted.

Other individuals who were far from the glare of the media spotlight but who contributed greatly to the unfolding of events were French president Jacques Chirac and Russian foreign minister Yevgeny Primakov. It was Chirac who developed the so-called UNSCOM Plus the Suits proposal that was ultimately used to break the impasse. But while Chirac was diligent in his determination to see the crisis resolved peacefully, Primakov played a much more controversial role in events. Praised for his mediation efforts in November 1997, at which time Iraq agreed to readmit the UNSCOM inspectors in return for Security Council reconsideration of the sanctions, his stock began to fall rapidly in early 1998. Primakov's friendship with his Iraqi counterpart Tariq Aziz had been considered a bonus just months earlier, but it began to attract suspicion when news of the possible weapons connection between Moscow and Baghdad broke. UNSCOM's first commissioner, Swede Rolf Ekeus, was quoted as saying that "You recognize every [Primakov] proposal has been prepared by Tariq [Aziz] . . . they match Iraq's ideas almost word by word, many times" (Smith 1998). Given widespread suspicion about the motives underlying other third-party efforts, it is not difficult to see why Annan gained quick credibility in Baghdad upon his arrival. His attempts to make balanced comments about the crisis were viewed very positively by the Iraqis, who had been at the receiving end of many negative UN appraisals of their position for many months, even years.

The Stakes

The standoff between Iraq and the United States dealt with issues critical to nation-states: sovereignty, autonomy, and security. For Iraq, suspicions that the United States was using its prominent position in UNSCOM as a front for spy operations were festering by 1997 (a charge given some credence when a link between UNSCOM and the Central Intelligence Agency was revealed in early 1999). Baghdad objected, in particular, to the number of Americans serving on UNSCOM inspection teams. It described the U.S.-piloted, but UN-sponsored, U-2 flights over Iraq as a hostile military threat from America. What had once seemed not to bother Saddam Hussein and his cohorts—the international pariah label affixed to Iraq—had apparently begun to take its toll. Tariq Aziz stuck doggedly to the position that sensitive sites such as the presidential palaces would not be subjected to UN inspections until sanctions were lifted and the disarmament file on Iraq closed.

For the United States, Iraq has been considered a serious national–security threat since its 1990 incursion into Kuwait and the ensuing discovery of alleged programs of weapons of mass destruction. Iraq's belligerence in refusing to go along with the agreement that ended the Gulf War has been a thorn in the sides of the Bush and Clinton administrations. The prospect of Iraq's stockpiling nerve agents such as anthrax and VX has provided the United States with its most serious contemporary threat to the security of its citizens—on the American mainland, where terrorism is now deeply feared, and abroad, where U.S. service personnel contend with Iraqi threats to shoot down the U-2 pilots and otherwise violently disrupt the monitoring of Iraq's activities.

But what is striking about the unfolding of this crisis is that Iraq's neighbors, the very nations that former U.S. Joint Chiefs of Staff chairman Colin Powell described as having "dialed 911 for the U.S." in 1990, were not voicing alarm about Baghdad's motivations (Ahrari and Starkey 1997, 145). This time, there seemed almost to be an impatience with the United States, a feeling that it needed to pick its fights more carefully. Indeed, suspicions of American motivations heightened after President Clinton was accused of having an affair with a White House intern and then trying to cover it up. This scandal opened the door all the way to accusations that the desire to shift the spotlight from his personal life might lead Clinton into a foreign adventure (the so-called *Wag the Dog* scenario). While the principle of Iraqi compliance with a treaty agreement did seem important to most of the concerned actors in the international system, so, too, did American credibility in the Middle East. Led by Jordan's foreign minister, Fayez Tarawneh, many regional actors began to draw parallels between Iraqi noncompliance with UN resolutions and what they deemed similar actions by Israel over time. Moreover, there seemed a feeling that the United States risked becoming an international bully if it continued to threaten force at every turn with Baghdad.

In addition to the trouble it was having winning international favor for its position during the crisis, the Clinton administration was also playing a very complicated game at home. Many in Congress—Republicans and Democrats alike—seemed in favor of strong action against Saddam Hussein and Iraq. In fact, Clinton had been criticized in November for accepting the Russian-brokered de-escalation proposal. However, after the White House intern scandal broke and Clinton began talking tougher about Iraq, there were rumblings from Republicans about the order of events. Moreover, the Republican-dominated Congress was generally highly skeptical of the UN and any mission that secretary-general Kofi Annan would run. So, by early February 1998, Clinton found himself in a classic "damned if I do, damned if I don't" position.

The Moves

To say that there was both a lack of trust and a lack of communication between the Americans and the Iraqis by February 1998 would be a serious understatement. In fact, strategically, both sides had set up for a dangerous game of chicken, where the first one to balk would be the loser. No real diplomacy was being conducted. It was a war of words and of escalating hostility; military action by one or both parties appeared imminent. The Iraqi government was keenly focused on preventing the inspection of sensitive sites in Baghdad, including the presidential palaces and various other governmental compounds. It was threatening to shoot down UN-sponsored overflights of Iraq, which U.S. pilots in American U-2 planes were conducting. Conversely, American interests and objectives in the situation were far less defined, as the administration was forced to admit in the wake of the Town Hall Meeting fiasco. The notion that Saddam Hussein could be bombed into adhering to the inspections regime was not sounding credible to critical observers around the world. With Iraqi civilians situated squarely in the middle of the intensifying crisis, the Clinton administration was faced with the frightening possibility of losing to Iraq in the court of international public opinion. The combination of these factors forced the United States to cede to the growing clamor for UN secretary-general Kofi Annan to inter-

Secretary-General Kofi Annan (center left) is greeted by Tariq Aziz (center right), deputy prime minister of Iraq, upon arriving at Saddam International Airport on a mission to resolve the weapons inspection crisis with Iraq (20 February 1998). UN/DPI photo by John Isaac.

vene in the situation as a mediator. But U.S. acceptance of the mission did not come easily. To go with its blessing, Annan had been told he would have to satisfy certain American conditions. Secretary of State Albright met with him in mid-February 1998 in New York and provided him with a list of dos and don'ts for the trip. It was agreed that the secretary-general would advance the "UNSCOM Plus" notion that President Chirac of France had developed. The suggestion was for diplomats of some sort—"suits"—from neutral countries to accompany the UNSCOM inspectors to sites deemed sensitive to the sovereignty of the Iraqi state. Of crucial importance to American acceptance of this compromise was what had been termed the snap-back option. This was an American demand that if Saddam Hussein broke the compliance pledge, this breach would "snap back and hit him with force" (Nelan 1998). The Americans were demanding that this notion be accepted by the other UN Security Council members in advance of Annan's trip and that it be included in any resolution that might result. Indeed, unbeknownst to the media covering the story at the time, the other members accepted this option before Annan flew off to Baghdad. Expectations that he would be able to stop the march toward a military encounter were low, but the secretary-general was able to beat the odds, or at least gain a reprieve.

Several factors account for the success that Annan achieved on his trip. First, he was able to negotiate directly with Saddam Hussein during his two days in Baghdad, rather than with deputies or other representatives. In fact, this was the first agreement in connection with the Gulf War and its aftermath that Saddam Hussein personally negotiated. Second, it seemed that both the Iraqi president and his deputy prime minister Tariq Aziz, the only other key figure in the negotiations on the Iraqi side, had developed a degree of trust in Annan's objectivity. This confidence is an essential attribute that any mediator must possess to be successful. Finally, as became clear in the comments Annan made after leaving Baghdad with an agreement in hand, he had successfully located the core of the issue for the Iraqi side. He used key words like dignity, sovereignty, and respect in his statement. He allowed that perhaps the UNSCOM inspectors had not previously respected the sensitivity of their mission, thereby lending some credence to the Iraqi accusation that the westerners on the teams had acted like "cowboys" in Baghdad. Annan even went so far as to praise Saddam Hussein for his willingness to negotiate and his "command of the facts" in the situation. But, ever the careful mediator, he also praised U.S. president Bill Clinton and his British counterpart Tony Blair for their skillful mixing of diplomacy with the threat of force (Rosenfeld 1998).

Annan was even more skillful in paving the way for American acceptance of the deal after he left Baghdad: timing was everything. Having telephoned Madeleine Albright from his guest house in Iraq after brokering the deal, he then declined to send her the final agreement during his stopover in Paris. He insisted that it should be presented for the first time to the full Security Council. Not to be denied a preview, U.S. intelligence sources found a bootleg copy of the agreement and delivered it to the White House early on the morning of Annan's return to New York (Nelan 1998, cited above). Nevertheless, the secretary-general had gained some valuable time, during which the advance press on the agreement suggested it was a reasonable one and should not be rejected out of hand by the Americans.

It is now clear, of course, that the Annan-brokered deal was a fragile one. Ten months later, in December 1998, Richard Butler reported that Iraq was still not complying with the weapons inspections and the United States and Britain launched the Desert Fox strikes on military installations in Iraq. The international response was mixed. Many voiced the opinion that Saddam Hussein had missed his opportunity to break out of the escalatory cycle he has been in for nearly a decade and had only himself to blame for the attacks. There were also, however, further indications that sympathy for the Iraqi people was continuing to rise. Many were critical of the UN decision to pull UNSCOM out of Iraq, believing that even the imperfect inspections process had been better than none. Moreover, not long after the air attacks were initiated, Butler announced that he would leave UNSCOM and Scott Ritter published a book criticizing the lack of resolve that all of Saddam Hussein's foes had shown over time. Kofi Annan's negotiations did not eliminate the many problems between the United States and Iraq, but he was able to demonstrate that diplomatic negotiation was viable as an alternative to war, even in this very contentious situation.

As was the case with the climate talks in Kyoto, victory in the court of international public opinion was very important to all parties to the Iraqi weapons inspections crisis. This may account for the ambiguous outcomes of both episodes, where each nation could claim victory by offering their own interpretations of the events during the negotiations, as well as the eventual conclusions.

Summary

In international relations and particularly within foreign policy analysis, negotiation is studied as a process specific to the system of states and crucial to its survival. *Negotiating a Complex World* utilizes a board game analogy to explain how the answers to various questions—who's involved, what's at stake, what kind of outcome is sought, and how it is sought—shape the international negotiation process. This chapter related two case examples to highlight the phases of international negotiation and to introduce many key concepts, including mediation, public goods, negotiation legacy, hostile diplomacy, positional bargaining, and iteration. These concepts, along with many others, will be further explored in the chapters to follow

Thematically, this book seeks to illustrate that diplomatic negotiation at the turn of this century is displaying many of the same characteristics and operating according to many of the same rules that it has since the 1700s.

Much attention is also devoted, however, to new and newly prominent facets of the international arena that are having a great impact on today's international negotiations. From the influence of new, nongovernmental global diplomats in the human rights and environmental areas to the much greater role domestic actors play in international affairs, state navigation of the international arena is a very complex endeavor.

Key Web Sites

International Campaign to Ban Landmines: http://www.icbl.org/
UN Framework Convention on Climate Change: http://www.unfccc.de/index.html
> (official site containing information about the post-Rio conferences of the parties and a list of country activities on climate change)

Global Warming at National Resources Defense Council (NRDC)-Dateline Kyoto: http://www.nrdc.org/field/kyoto.html
> ("diary entries" for each day of the conference from NRDC representatives to the talks)

National Public Radio (NPR) Report on U.S. vice president Al Gore in Kyoto: http://www.npr.org/ramfiles/971208.atc.10.ram
> (a RealAudio file from NPR's *All Things Considered* on December 8, 1997)

UNSCOM: http://www.un.org/Depts/unscom/
> (official site of UNSCOM)

U.S. Institute of Peace Iraq Crisis Links: http://www.usip.org/library/regions/iraq.html
> (a collection of links highlighting the background and various elements of the crisis)

Iraq Arms Inspection Crisis Overview: http://www.nytimes.com/library/world/iraq-index.html
> (*New York Times* International Issues in Depth. Other special features are available at http://www.nytimes.com/library/world/index-specials.html.)

Transcript of Ohio State University Town Hall Meeting: http://secretary.state.gov/www/statements/1998/980218.html

NPR Report on the Ohio State University Town Hall Meeting: http://www.npr.org/ramfiles/980218.atc.11.ram
> (a RealAudio file from NPR's *All Things Considered* on February 18, 1998)

All of the above sites can be directly accessed from the web site for this book: http://www.icons.umd.edu/negotiating/links.htm

2

The Board

No two negotiations are the same. Even when the same actors return to the negotiation table to discuss the very same issue for a second time, both the dynamics and the results may be quite different. Identifying the particular mix of factors involved helps explain why negotiations take the twists and turns that they do. This chapter first examines the international system setting in which all negotiations take place and then offers a detailed checklist of characteristics that distinguish individual negotiation situations. Taken together, the international system setting and the specific negotiation characteristics can be conceptualized as the board upon which the strategic game of negotiation is played.

This negotiation board, or the context in which the negotiations take place, must be examined from both a macro and a micro perspective. The larger picture is the international system setting in which the power relations among actors—the system configuration—and the relative stability of that configuration are particularly important. Once this overall shape has been laid out, it is possible to look in detail at individual negotiation episodes and identify their key characteristics, including such factors as the number of parties to the negotiation, the types of issues involved, and the level of commitment by the parties. An examination of the way these factors play out allows one to appreciate the strategic decisions the parties make, and to understand why some negotiation strategies are more effective than others.

Consider again the U.S.–Iraqi situation, when on August 2, 1990, Iraqi forces invaded Kuwait and occupied the emirate within six hours. During the course of the next four months, the United States was able to negotiate the mobilization of an almost universal coalition of nations that committed to sending troops and materiel, provided airbases and troop deployment facilities, and guaranteed financial support. In short, this coalition presented a united world front in the face of Iraqi aggression. Six years later, the United States was faced once again with Iraqi defiance of world opinion: Iraq denied access to UN weapons inspectors carrying out a Security Council mandate to search for evidence of chemical and biological warfare preparations. This time, however, U.S. negotiators could muster only the active support of Britain. Moreover, they were denied landing and staging rights by virtually all of the Gulf states and received none of the financial and moral backing that had typified the earlier confrontation. What had changed in this relatively short period of time? The answer lies in the configuration of the international system in which these two episodes occurred and the relations among the system units—the board upon which these critical events transpired and the negotiations they fostered.

The International System

As the twenty-first century dawns, negotiators face an international environment that has changed remarkably since the turn of the previous century. The number of sovereign states has grown from fewer than 50 to nearly 200, and myriad intergovernmental, nongovernmental, and transnational entities clutter the landscape. Citizen diplomacy, the information revolution, and the power of multinational business enterprises, whose influence can exceed that of many small states, have all combined to create a global arena wherein negotiation skills are essential.

While it is true that all of these factors and institutions have become increasingly relevant, it is still the case that the international system setting is typically described in terms of its central units—sovereign states—and the power relations among them. At the time of the first episode with Iraq, immediately following the end of the cold war, the United States was emerging as the single dominant power in the international system, the USSR having lost control over its alliance partners in central and eastern Europe. In fact, the USSR itself was soon to dissolve into thirteen independent republics. Under these conditions, the states in the international system were scrambling to be counted among the trusted allies of what appeared to be the dominant power: the United States. By January–February 1998, these relationships had largely sorted themselves out. While the United States was still in a dominant position militarily, it was clear by then that weaker states did not necessarily need to blindly follow the U.S. lead. Even Saudi Arabia and the United Arab Emirates, two of the staunchest members of the anti-Iraq coalition of 1990–1991, refused to fall into step with the United States the next time around.

Polarity

The distribution of power among states is most commonly referred to as polarity. Both the number of poles in a system and the way power is distributed among them characterize the types of international systems. Five different international systems or polar structures, along with two extremely bloody, anarchic systems corresponding to the two world wars, have characterized the twentieth century (see box below).

Polar Structures in the Twentieth Century

Balance of power (to 1914): A relatively small number of nation-states operated in a system whereby shifting alliances kept any single state from developing a preponderance of power.

World War I (1914–1918): a breakdown of the balance of power, a result of the crumbling of existing alliances rather than the repeated shifting that had kept the nation-states in balance before 1914.

Multipolarity (1918–1939): a diffusion of military power and political decision making among a small group of relatively equal units; isolation practices among major powers.

World War II (1939–1945): an outgrowth of isolationism, which allowed aggressive powers to grow unchecked and become global security threats.

Bipolarity (1945–1962): a concentration of military power and political decision making in two relatively equal preeminent states— the United States and the USSR—and two very rigid military alliances—the North Atlantic Treaty Organization (NATO) and the Warsaw Pact.

Polycentrism (1963–1989): a hybrid structure, with the United States and the USSR continuing to constitute two centers of military power but with multiple centers of political decision making.

Unipolarity (1990–): an overwhelming concentration of military capability in one entity—the United States clearly is the military hegemon—although political power is even more diffuse than it was under polycentrism.

One way to highlight the impact of international system structure or polarity on the negotiation process is to examine a particular long-term conflict that spans two or more of these historical systems and involves a number of negotiation episodes along the way. The Arab–Israeli conflict, stretching from the end of World War II to the present, provides such an unfortunate example. The "return" of the Jews to the "Land of Israel" (Palestine), beginning in the 1880s and increasing after the Holocaust, provides the backdrop for this conflict. It was, however, the November 1947 General Assembly resolution calling for the partition of Palestine into separate Arab and Jewish states, and the eventual unilateral proclamation of the State of Israel in 1948, that triggered this protracted conflict. Significant negotiation episodes produced cease-fires and disengagement agreements following each of the twenty-five international crises that have punctuated this long-standing conflict between Israel and its Arab neighbors (Brecher and Wilkenfeld 1997).

Early Arab–Israeli negotiations occurred during the immediate post–World War II bipolar period, highlighted by the emerging strength of the Soviet Union, as well as the last gasps of France and the United Kingdom as sources of power and influence. In fact, the negotiations ending both the 1948–1949 and 1956 wars found the United States and the USSR working together to resolve these conflicts. However, by 1956 it was clear that the two superpowers diverged on a number of key elements in Middle East policy. Because of these disagreements, by 1970 and 1973—when Israel, Egypt, and Syria engaged in all-out military conflict—these states served as virtual proxies for the two superpowers. Finally, with the end of the cold war and the demise of the Soviet Union, yet another transformation occurred in the structure of the international system. The shift to unipolarity has affected the Arab–Israeli conflict and, for that matter, other conflict arenas in the Middle East. The United States, for example, is extensively engaged in Israeli–Palestinian negotiations (see Wye River box in chapter 5), whereas Russia and the UN are involved only marginally.

Crisis

Besides being affected by the existing structure of the international system, international negotiations are also characterized by the climate in which they are conducted. Of particular importance to negotiators is the impact of crisis. Since crises often act as catalysts for major system change, they represent a wild card that is capable of changing the shape of the international system and altering the outcomes of individual negotiation episodes. The extent to which national actors perceive themselves to be in a crisis can have an impact on the pace of the negotiations and the range of alternatives examined, as well as on the types of outcomes that result (treaties, interim agreements, unstable cease-fires).

From the larger system perspective, an international crisis can be defined as an increase in the intensity of hostile interactions between states. This change carries with it a heightened probability of military hostility that, in turn, destabilizes their relationship in ways that threaten the stability of a regional subsystem or the entire international system. The Berlin Crisis of 1948, the Cuban Missile Crisis of 1962, and the 1973 Middle East War were all instances in which critical negotiations occurred in crisis environments.

> **KEY TERM**
>
> **International Crisis** An increase in the intensity of hostile interactions among states, with a heightened probability of military action.

From the point of view of a particular state and its decision makers, a crisis occurs when the leaders of a country perceive a threat to basic values (territory, population, economy), an awareness of finite response time (it will not go away unless some action is taken), and a heightened probability of involvement in military hostilities (Brecher and Wilkenfeld 1997). Perhaps the essence of crisis at the national level is captured by the stress levels the key decision makers experience—for example, Harry S. Truman in 1948, as he grappled with the Soviet blockade of Berlin; John F. Kennedy in 1962, as he maneuvered for the removal of Soviet missiles from Cuba; and Golda Meir and Anwar Sadat in 1973–1974, as they attempted to wrest maximum advantage in the negotiations that followed the Yom Kippur War.

From the perspective of negotiation, the three key elements of crisis are threat, time pressure, and the accompanying stress that these engender. Neither the Kyoto environmental conference in 1997 nor the Uruguay Round of General Agreement on Tariffs and Trade (GATT) talks from 1986 to 1994 was characterized by the need for immediate resolution. Indeed, each was a stage in an ongoing and complex negotiation. On the other hand, the Gulf crisis of 1997–early 1998 posed a serious challenge for negotiators; as deadlines approached, stress levels rose, massive troop movements took place, and the probability of military hostilities increased. Negotiations conducted in an atmosphere of threat and stress, accompanied by time pressures and deadlines, can often put decision makers in positions where they cannot fully explore options or take advantage of alternative information sources, thus leading to the possibility that less-than-optimal decisions will be made.

There are circumstances in which routine negotiations take on some of the characteristics of a crisis environment. When the delegates to the Kyoto climate change conference first gathered in 1997, after years of preparation following the Rio conference of 1992, the negotiation environment was routine. However, as the official end of the conference neared and it appeared that little in the way of an agreement would result, U.S. president Clinton dispatched Vice President Gore to Kyoto to convey an increased sense of urgency in the hope that it would spur the delegates into action. Soon, an atmosphere of crisis (nonmilitary, to be sure) gripped the participants, and both real and imagined deadlines pushed the negotiators toward the text of a treaty that would reflect at least some progress. In fact, the official end of the meeting was pushed back a day to enable the delegates to make some demonstrable progress.

Conversely, skilled negotiators, often with the help of mediators and third parties (see discussion below), can sometimes transform an atmosphere of crisis into a routine negotiation environment. By eliminating or at least reducing the perception of threat and limited time, thereby lowering the stress levels that these entail, the negotiation can be transformed into a positive environment more conducive to the examination of alternatives and the achievement of a mutually beneficial outcome. In late 1995, at the height of the three-year-old war in Bosnia, President Clinton invited the presidents of Bosnia, Croatia, and Serbia to a conference in Dayton, Ohio. The issues at this conference involved territory, a constitution for Bosnia, withdrawal of forces to cease-fire lines, and the deployment of a NATO peacekeeping force. Removed from the extreme crisis atmosphere of ethnic cleansing, massive civilian casualties, and severe damage to the infrastructure of Bosnia, the leaders were ultimately able to negotiate the Dayton Peace Accords under intense U.S. mediation and bring that phase of the armed conflict to a close.

Third-Party Intervention

> **KEY TERM**
>
> **Third-Party Intervention**
> The introduction of an external party into a negotiation when it is apparent that progress cannot be achieved without some form of outside involvement.

Like polarity and crisis, the intervention of a third party into particular conflicts or negotiations also represents a system-level factor that can significantly affect the progress of a specific negotiation episode. Third parties usually enter into a negotiation when it is apparent that progress cannot be achieved without some form of outside involvement. In certain crisis situations, usually when a local crisis threatens to widen dramatically, third parties intervene to defuse conflict or to prevent it from spreading and further destabilizing the region or international system. The availability of third parties to mediate in international negotiation situations can have important ramifications in terms of how the negotiations play out and their ultimate success or failure.

Major powers and small states; representatives of regional, global, or security organizations; private citizens; religious organizations; and special interest groups have all played important roles in international negotiations in recent years (see box below). On some occasions, this third-party mediation effort can result in both a resolution of the conflict situation and a broadening of the role of the original mediating party—for example, the continued U.S. involvement in Bosnia in the form of peacekeeping troops in the region under the terms of the Dayton Accord,

Types of International Mediation

Mediation by global organization: on behalf of the UN, Count Folke Bernadotte, and later UN under-secretary-general Ralph Bunche, played important mediation roles in the negotiations leading to the 1948–1949 Arab–Israeli armistice agreements.

Mediation by regional organization: the failed attempt by representatives of the EU to mediate the conflict in Bosnia, 1992–1995.

Mediation by private citizen: former U.S. president Jimmy Carter conducted private mediation in negotiations surrounding the Haiti crisis of 1994 and the North Korean nuclear crisis of 1994.

Mediation by religious organization: the Vatican played an important role in 1984 in mediating the so-called Beagle Channel dispute between Chile and Argentina.

Mediation by special interest group: the Ford Foundation financed a 1991 UN peace initiative to end El Salvador's civil war.

or the UN-mediated cease-fires in the Middle East that have resulted in the long-term stationing of UN troops along Israel's borders with its Arab neighbors over the past fifty years. Other instances of mediation are more short-lived—for example, the very effective but limited role that Algeria played in helping resolve the Iran hostage crisis of 1979–1980.

Third-party intervention, or mediation, as it is often referred to, has been defined by Young (1968, 34) as "any action taken by an actor that is not a direct party to the crisis, that is designed to reduce or remove one or more of the problems of the bargaining relationship and, therefore, to facilitate the termination of the crisis." Bobrow (1981, 188) speaks of the positive contributions of third parties as "focusing the parties on a particular termination agreement, devising a formula to avoid hard issues, providing an agenda, and manipulating timing." Third parties can also provide face-saving mechanisms for the conflicting parties by creating opportunities and excuses for what the parties would like to do anyway but might find politically difficult. Raiffa (1982, 108–109) indicates that third-party intervention can help in the following ways: by bringing parties together; establishing a constructive ambiance for negotiation; collecting and judiciously communicating selected confidential material; helping parties to clarify their values; deflating unreasonable claims and loosening commitments; seeking joint gains; keeping negotiations going; and articulating the rationale for agreement.

A mediator, at least in theory, should be neutral across the parties involved, even though this characteristic is not always in evidence or even possible in contemporary international affairs. It should be noted that mediation is not the same as arbitration, the latter being a judicial process where the third-party issues a ruling and the parties are authoritatively bound to abide by that ruling. By contrast, "mediation is a noncoercive, nonviolent, and ultimately, nonbinding form of intervention" (Bercovitch 1997, 127). Depending upon the situation, however, the line between mediation and arbitration can be blurred at the bargaining table.

A mediator's motives for intervening in a conflict or intractable negotiation will affect his or her ability to achieve some form of resolution. Aside from the temporal benefits of helping international actors resolve conflict, third parties get involved because on some level they have interests at stake in the negotiation and wish to facilitate peaceful resolution of the problems engendered in that negotiation (Zartman and Touval 1996, 446). However, a closer examination of the third-party interests at stake sometimes turns up a darker side of intervention, wherein third parties intervene in negotiations in order to further their own special interests. Many of the interventions that have taken place in Africa in recent years have been designed to support and strengthen one of the parties to the dispute rather than to bring about a mediated settlement that is mutually beneficial. Hoping to derive ideological gain, Cuba maintained a significant military presence in Angola from the mid-1970s to the early 1990s, siding with the Marxist-oriented Popular Movement for the Liberation of Angola (MPLA) against the South African–backed National Union for the Total Independence of Angola (UNITA). In 1994, France dispatched a military force to Rwanda in a nonneutral intervention to support the Hutu-led government against the Tutsi Rwanda Patriotic Front—in this instance, to enhance France's influence in Africa. In the extreme, such interventions have resulted in territorial or economic gain for the intervening party.

Negotiation Characteristics: A Checklist

Having reviewed the larger international system setting that functions as a backdrop for individual negotiations, it is now useful to examine the specific characteristics of individual negotiation episodes. Basically, one can approach a negotiation with a series of questions in hand—for example, how many actors are involved, is there linkage among negotiation issues, or is there a deadline by which the talks must conclude? The following checklist focuses on three aspects of negotiation: actor, issue, and process characteristics. Taken in combination, these factors define the structure of the episode (the board) and help determine the strategic approach that makes the most sense for the involved actors. Understanding these characteristics and how they intertwine to affect the outcomes of negotiations should prove helpful, whether one is analyzing historical negotiation episodes or developing new negotiation strategies.

Actor Characteristics

Number of Actors/Coalitions

It is commonplace to think of negotiations in terms of two-party inter-actions. Whether it is a husband and a wife, a buyer and a seller, or two nations on the verge of war, this is the model through which it is easiest to conceptualize the give-and-take of the negotiation process. Yet many negotiations in both the domestic and international realms involve more than two actors, and often this adds complexity far in excess of the actual number of additional players at the negotiation table.

It is important to distinguish the issue of number of actors in the nego-tiation from the question of how unified a specific negotiation team is internally. It is equally important to distinguish a multiactor case from a two-actor negotiation where a third actor takes the role of mediator, as dis-cussed above. This latter situation is still a variant of the two-actor nego-tiation model, albeit one with facilitation.

As the number of actors increases from two to many, the fundamental dynamics of the process itself are altered. Most signifi-cantly, the possibility of coalition formation between two or more of the actors means that there is now a negotiation within a nego-tiation. Often, the formation of a coalition has the effect of reducing the number of actors back down to two, and therefore to a

> ### KEY TERM
>
> **Coalition**   A collection of actors who band together to try to achieve common goals, at either the domestic or transnational level.

more familiar and manageable model for the participants. On occasion, such coalitions are inherently unstable—take, for example, the three domi-nant coalitions in the UN during the height of the cold war: the capitalist West, the socialist Soviet bloc, and the Group of 77 nonaligned states. In fact, one of the first signs that the international system was evolving in the early 1960s from a bipolar to a polycentric system with looser alliance structures was the lessening of bloc voting behavior in the UN. The broad coalition the United States formed at the height of the 1990–1991 Gulf crisis represented a triumph of expediency and self-interest over ideology, whereas the inabil-ity of the United States to re-create that unanimity during the Gulf crisis of early 1998 attested to a significantly changed international atmosphere.

Coalition ties can provide added clout by allowing an actor to rely explicitly or implicitly on the power of allies to enhance a negotiation position. However, a tight alliance structure may also restrict the maneu-vering room available to negotiators by reducing the range of alternative negotiated outcomes that will be acceptable not only to them but to their coalition partners. The tightness of the U.S.–Israeli alliance has meant that the range of outcomes that the United States can explore with the Palestinians on Israel's behalf is highly restricted.

Hopmann (1996) argues that multiparty or multilateral negotiations exhibit greater complexity because of the possibility of coalition formation, crosscutting cleavages, and the possibility of group dynamics intervening in the process. At the very least, the involvement of multiple parties means an increase in the complexity of the negotiation. With each party to the negotiation seeking a different outcome, and each viewing the negotiation with a different sense of urgency, the possibilities for both delay and failure are enhanced.

Team Cohesion

Ideally, all members of a negotiation team have reached consensus about the issue under discussion before they sit down at the table. This model of a negotiation team generally involves a leader or chief negotiator, with other members of the team possessing specific expertise (legal, economic, military). In such cases, it will be common for the team leader to do most of the talking, and for that person to seek the advice and expertise of other delegation members, as appropriate. Under this model, one would expect that the delegation as a whole will be able to present a unified position during the course of the negotiations. This can be described as a monolithic model.

KEY TERM

Monolithic Model   The assumption that all members of a negotiating team are working to advance the same interests and speak with one voice.

However, negotiation actors "are not only those negotiating 'across the table' (horizontally). Parties also negotiate within the team at the table or in caucus. Negotiations also occur between the 'table team members' and their respective decision makers (vertical authority), and also within the vertical authority as it attempts to decide upon directions to give the team" (Colosi 1986, 245). Thus, at the other extreme might be a model in which, although there is still a delegation leader, there are also other individual members of status equal to the leader and possessing somewhat divergent goals. Or, while the delegation head has overall authority, that person must defer to others on specific issues during the course of the negotiation; this is different from simply seeking advice and expertise in the monolithic model above. In fact, the delegation might reflect the types of cleavages present in the government itself or in the society as a whole. We may even find instances where there is some uncertainty about who the actual negotiating partner is: during the complex negotiations over the U.S. Embassy hostages held in Iran from 1979 to 1981, the United States was not certain that the group with which it was negotiating did in fact represent those who were actually holding the hostages. Such delegations often reflect the failure of one of the teams to reach a consensus position prior to departure for the negotiation session. While this phenomenon is most common to countries with a highly bureaucratic foreign policy apparatus—the United States, for example—it also occurs in more centralized systems, where the interests of competing elites must be attended to. This is the heterogeneous model.

> ### KEY TERM
>
> **Heterogeneous Model** The assumption that the different members of a negotiating team hold different interests, which may be in conflict with one another.

These two models represent extremes, and most often negotiation teams include elements of both. There may be issues on which there is broad team consensus and on which the delegation can act in a unified manner, as well as issues on which there is sharp disagreement within the team. In the case of Israel's complex negotiations with the Palestinians, no member of an Israeli government delegation would be willing to make territorial concessions involving a radical change in the status of Jerusalem. At the same time, there might be differences within the delegation over the size and timing of Israeli withdrawals from occupied territory on the West Bank, reflecting the deep cleavages in Israel's government and population in general. This same dynamic was evident in the case of successive American delegations to the Strategic Arms Limitation Talks (SALT). Delegations were composed of specialists from the Departments of State and Defense, and while they agreed on the need to reduce arms, they often reflected the sharp differences within the government itself over the political and military aspects of U.S. relations with the USSR during the height of the cold war.

Actor Capabilities

The first part of chapter 2 illustrates the ways that power relations at the international system level (bipolarity, multipolarity, etc.) define the larger setting in which the negotiations take place and impact the options available to the actors in the negotiation. In the present instance, the concern is with the ways the relative capabilities of individual actors affect the course of the negotiation and its ultimate outcome. Since it is rare that all parties to a negotiation have equal power, conventional wisdom assumes that stronger actors will drive the better bargain and end up with the lion's share; conversely, weaker actors have less clout and therefore get the shorter end of the negotiation stick. However, strength is often a matter of perception, as evidenced by the fact that power relations are among the murkier concepts in social science. In international relations, not only is there great difficulty in reaching consensus on what constitutes national capability, but the problem is further confounded by discussion of measurement issues. In the increasingly complex international environment of the twenty-first century, different elements of power will come to the fore under varying circumstances—military, economic, political, territorial, demographic. The issue is how and when the various aspects of power impact on the course and ultimate outcome of a negotiation.

Limits to Power

Power is situational. To understand this fact, one need only think back to the horrifying pictures of U.S. Marines removing the bodies of over 200 dead comrades after a 1983 suicide bombing destroyed their barracks in Beirut; the sight of an American troop carrier under siege in the harbor of Port-au-Prince, Haiti, in 1994; or to the helplessness of the world's five declared nuclear powers as first India and then Pakistan detonated underground nuclear devices in 1998. The mere possession of over-whelming military power does not necessarily mean that it can be effectively and fully exercised in the pursuit of national goals.

At the negotiation table, power intertwines with commitment and opportunity to create unique, and sometimes unexpected, dynamics. The Paris Peace Agreements, under which the United States formalized its withdrawal from Vietnam, was a classic case of commitment and resolve winning out over "objective" power. The stark pictures of U.S. helicopters plucking the last of the American staff and their South Vietnamese collaborators from the rooftop of the U.S. Embassy in Saigon, while those left behind clamored desperately to get inside the embassy compound, pointed to the final humiliation in a decade-long struggle that the United States had conducted with itself over the disconnect of power, commitment, and resolve.

History shows that preponderant power cannot always be effectively exercised during negotiations. For example, the possession of nuclear weapons does not necessarily afford a means of achieving advantage in a negotiation. Only if a nuclear power can actually convince the other side that such weapons will be used in pursuit of the objectives under negotiation will such capability make a difference. North Vietnam did not believe that the United States would use tactical nuclear weapons on the battlefield, largely because of the impact of such a decision on the Soviet Union's position in the conflict. In fact, the deployment of U.S. long-range bombers to flatten significant portions of North Vietnam had the unintended effect of hardening the resolve of the North and making it even less flexible at the negotiating table. Hence, the United States was effectively stripped of its nuclear capability at the Paris negotiations—its credibility was hopelessly compromised—and the gap in power between the United States and North Vietnam was thereby narrowed dramatically. The United States learned a costly lesson in Vietnam about the limits to power.

Mobs of South Vietnamese try to scale the 14-foot wall of the U.S. Embassy in Saigon, April 29, 1975. (AP Photo/files)

Actor Norms

National negotiation teams differ widely in terms of the norms that they bring to the table. As will be apparent in chapter 3, some cultures stress the need for clear-cut victory, while others value the achievement of consensus and a mutually beneficial outcome. U.S. negotiators, for example, are known for a laissez-faire attitude toward planning, "cowboy" shoot-out techniques, demands for rapid action, and even excessive legalism. Their sense of independence, desire for individual achievement, and personal drive for success are all reflected in their behavior in the negotiation setting. Japanese and other East Asian cultures, evolving from the general beliefs and social structures of the Confucian system, tend to bring a different set of values and norms to the negotiation setting: dependence, trust, reticence, hierarchy, obligation, loyalty, and harmony. It should be obvious that these two very different approaches translate into very different styles of negotiation.

These two approaches can be differentiated by labeling them low-context (individualistic) and high-context (relationship-oriented) negotiating styles (R. Cohen 1997). Under this generalized rubric, Americans—representing a classic low-context culture—exhibit a style grounded in a belief that a person can "freely manipulate his environment for his own purposes" (Mushakoji 1976, 45–46, as cited in R. Cohen). Results, rather than relationships, are the key. On the other hand, the Japanese—representing a classic high-context culture—exhibit an adaptive style. Negotiation is not an end in itself, but an episode in a long-term relationship to be built between the parties. The clash of low-context and high-context cultures at the bargaining table can create serious problems in communication and, ultimately, in negotiators' ability to reach agreements.

Clearly, as states acquire more information about the negotiation styles of others, they will adapt their approaches where possible. This, in turn, is leading to what many students of negotiation are calling a culture of negotiation, which entails a language, style, and approach that nations share while negotiating, and which washes out many aspects of individual styles.

Actor Commitment

Actors involved in a negotiation may also differ in terms of their commitment to the issues under discussion. Just as on the playing field or battlefield, where differences in the degree of commitment of the parties can sometimes make up for more objectively measured power differentials, so, too, can variations in commitment strengthen or weaken hands at the negotiation table. These differences, of course, can be real or perceived. During the protracted Vietnam conflict, it was clear from the outset that the relative commitments of the United States and North Vietnam were heavily influenced by the differences in the conflict's immediacy for the populations of the two countries. The U.S. administration was never able to effectively convey the strategic importance of South Vietnam to the American people to the same degree that the North Vietnamese government was able to for its own population. The North Vietnamese negotiators in Paris certainly took the growing domestic dissent in the United States and the erosion of public support for the American role in Vietnam as signs of weakening U.S. commitment to its negotiating positions and hence were encouraged to hold out for larger concessions.

While the Vietnam War and its negotiated termination offers an example of the impact of both the limits to power and a weakening American commitment, the behavior of the United States in the tense negotiations surrounding the Cuban Missile Crisis shows a much different pattern. In that 1962 crisis, the United States was able to demonstrate a credible threat to use the ultimate in force at its disposal and to couple that threat with a demonstrable commitment to the particular conflict issue. Ultimately, the USSR backed off, unwilling to exercise the necessary power and unable to demonstrate an overwhelming commitment to the issue in dispute.

More recently, the AOSIS, a key player at the Kyoto climate negotiations, offered another example of how intense commitment can provide a compelling substitute for actual power in influencing a negotiation outcome. This coalition of forty-two small island nations from around the world was formed in 1994 to ensure that the needs of its members would be heard amid the clamor from the vastly more powerful states in the climate negotiations. Working in conjunction with two NGOs—Earth Kind and Counterpart International—AOSIS crafted a program of action for Kyoto and achieved prominence at the negotiations with its argument that rising sea levels would spell disaster and death for island populations around the world if concerted action were not taken soon (Alliance of Small Island States 1997).

An important factor to bear in mind is that, over a period of time, the same adversaries may face off across a negotiating table over different issues (see discussion of legacy below) and that power and commitment levels do not necessarily remain constant across issue areas. Six years before the Cuban Missile Crisis, the United States failed to demonstrate sufficient resolve as Soviet troops and armor rolled into Hungary; nor did it keep the Soviets from similar action in Czechoslovakia in the Prague Spring crisis of 1968.

Issue Characteristics

Number of Issues/Bargaining Dimensions

Besides the variations attributable to the number of actors involved, negotiations can be characterized by the number of issues in contention among those actors. Like the addition of actors to a negotiation, an increase in the number of issues clearly expands the complexity of the negotiation. However, an increase in issues can also enhance the probability of a successful outcome to the negotiations since the number of combinations of favorable outcomes for each of the actors to consider is increased. In effect, as the number of issues increases, the situation has the potential to change from one where a single actor wins and the

> **KEY TERM**
>
> **Zero-Sum** A situation where one player can gain only at the expense of the other player—when one player wins, the other necessarily loses.

other loses (zero-sum) to a more mutually beneficial one that offers opportunities for each actor to win something.

The zero-sum case is characterized by a single issue in contention, such as territory, where the two actors have strictly opposing interests. The more one actor gets, the less the other gets (Raiffa 1982, 133). Another variant involves one actor's holding all of a territory in dispute, while the other has no access to it at all. Many of the most intractable international conflicts can be seen as zero-sum bargaining cases over territory: India and Pakistan over Kashmir, Ethiopia and Eritrea over a disputed border region, the Israelis and the Palestinians over the West Bank. The apparent simplicity of the "winner takes all" bargaining situation is also its inherent weakness when it comes to negotiating a resolution. With only one issue in contention, one actor will always win, while the other will always lose.

KEY TERM

Non–Zero-Sum A situation where it is possible for all players to be "winners"; the possibility of mutual gains.

By contrast, if there are several issues to negotiate, the two parties can often move into a non–zero-sum environment. Now they are no longer strict competitors. As Raiffa notes: "It is no longer true that if one party gets more, the other necessarily has to get less: they can both get more. They can cooperate in order to change the pie that they eventually will have to divide" (1982, 131). In the fall of 1962, the United States and the USSR were locked in what was ultimately the most dangerous superpower confrontation of the cold war over the issue of Soviet installation of nuclear missiles in Cuba, only ninety miles from the U.S. mainland. Initially, the confrontation involved the single issue of American insistence on the immediate withdrawal of the missiles. As the crisis continued, and military action seemed inevitable, the United States gradually expanded the issue set to include the status of U.S. missiles stationed in Turkey and targeted at the USSR, as well as the question of an American invasion of the island of Cuba itself. This expansion of the issue set had the effect of allowing the USSR to commit to the withdrawal of the missiles from Cuba and, nevertheless, to be able to claim victory on the latter two issues. In essence, both parties emerged from the negotiation with some degree of victory.

Skilled negotiators, often with the help of mediators, can transform a "winner takes all" bargaining situation into one with opportunities for mutual benefit. Once this happens, it is possible for both actors to come away from the negotiation feeling that they won on at least some issues. In 1996–1997, Israel and the Palestinian Authority were locked in a seemingly unresolvable dispute over Israel's pullout from Hebron on the West Bank, the last major Arab city from which Israel was to withdraw as part of the Oslo Accords of 1993. U.S. mediators were able to expand the issue set from a narrow focus on territory to one that encompassed additional issues, such as security arrangements and access to holy places, so that it was possible for both parties to see benefit and thereby move toward an eventual agreement.

Issue Linkage

Related to the number of issues is the question of whether there are linkage effects. One manifestation of linkage occurs when a negotiation that a nation conducts with an actor is tied to similar negotiations it is also conducting with that actor. For example, in 1998, as President Clinton prepared to make the first presidential visit to China since that

> **KEY TERM**
>
> **Linkage** The inclusion of additional issues not directly related to the issue under negotiation.

country's government's violent repression of pro-democracy student demonstrations in Tiananmen Square in 1989, it was clear that the standards to which the United States was holding China in the area of human rights were not the same as those it was applying to other nations with which it was then negotiating. While human rights groups and others cried foul, the United States was following a policy of expediency, wherein it applied standards in a differential manner, depending upon overall American foreign policy objectives. In this case, the U.S. position on human rights violations in China appeared to be linked (some would say held hostage) to the U.S. economic desire to capitalize on the vast Chinese markets.

But linkage and the U.S.–China case can be looked at from a second perspective, one that is perhaps more generous to the United States. The United States, of course, is pursuing multiple goals simultaneously as it interacts with the Chinese government. While the U.S. government is interested in moving China toward a more acceptable standard of human rights practices in its society, it has important economic interests in China as well. By attempting to create linkages between progress on human rights and the achievement of "most favored nation" status (recently termed "normal trade relations" by the Clinton administration) as an economic trading partner, the United States hopes to move both issues in a favorable direction for both countries. Indeed, this second aspect of linkages brings us back to our discussion of the mutually beneficial bargaining perspective—and to the means nations have at their disposal to transform difficult and even deadlocked negotiations into ones with the possibility of mutually beneficial outcomes for all.

Time Frame

In the discussion of the international system setting (above), the time factor was explored as one of the distinguishing characteristics of a crisis, in that the actors in a crisis negotiation often perceive that there is a finite or limited time for response. In international crises involving military–security issues, time is often coupled with the possibility of violence, in the sense that as real or perceived deadlines approach, resorting to violence is increasingly seen as the only available alternative. But even in routine situations, and in instances where the alternative to not achieving agreement in some time frame need not be violence, time pressures nevertheless exert their own influences on the negotiation process.

The time factor does not necessarily affect all negotiation actors equally. Consider, for example, the long, drawn-out Israeli–Palestinian negotiations involving the conditions under which Israel would undertake a pullback from territories it has occupied in the West Bank since 1967. Assuming there is value to Israel from continued occupation of these territories, it has no particular incentive to move quickly in these negotiations, even though it continues to pay a heavy price in terms of violence against its own citizens and in the court of world public opinion. The Palestinians, on the other hand, given the context of the power struggle between Yasir Arafat and the Palestinian Authority, as well as with the more militant Hamas, feel pressure to bring this matter to a hasty and successful conclusion—or else Arafat risks losing power to Hamas. From this perspective, the incentives for Israel are to move slowly; for the Palestinians, they are to move quickly.

However, for Israel, there is a modest incentive to strengthen Arafat and his colleagues because the alternative prospect of negotiating with Hamas is not appealing. Thus, Israel may be inclined to speed things up under these circumstances. On the other hand, slowing down allows it to continue to create "facts on the ground" in the form of new settlements and increased settler population, making it more and more difficult for Israel to make concessions to the Palestinians. So not only does time function differently for the two parties, but even within a single negotiation party there are often conflicting perceptions of the role that time plays.

Time, in the form of deadlines, may be real or artificial. Real deadlines exist in hostage situations, when treaties are about to expire, and when actual or impending natural disasters require concerted effort on the part of members of the international community. Deadlines are more artificial or flexible when all that is at stake is the changing of travel plans or the rescheduling of meetings between important leaders. There is a maxim to the effect that 90 percent of the negotiation takes place in the last 10 percent of the time allowed, emphasizing the importance of mutually credible deadlines (Colosi 1986).

It is critical for negotiators to gain an accurate understanding of the different ways in which time impacts on the parties to the negotiation. In some instances, time can be bundled as part of the negotiated outcome, so that the ultimate agreement reflects one party's need for a time-sensitive resolution, while the party with less time pressure may be able to gain other types of concessions. Israel, for example, sees considerable value in what has been termed a phased pullback in the West Bank, under which it can periodically check on the Palestinians' compliance with their end of the bargain before making further concessions. The Palestinians, for their part, get to demonstrate to their constituency that through the negotiation process, some tangible gains have been made in terms of the restoration of territory. In this instance, time and security have been bundled as part of a mutually beneficial bargaining process, thus creating the

Figure 2.1 The Oslo Accords: Proposed Implementation

potential for each party to come away from the negotiation in a position to point to positive gains.

Process Characteristics

Public or Private Forum

Another way in which negotiations can be characterized has to do with whether they are conducted in private or public forums. In actual fact, we almost never see pure cases of either, although some come pretty close. When U.S. secretary of state Henry Kissinger held his famous news conference in Beijing in 1971, announcing that the United States and the People's Republic of China (PRC) had just negotiated the opening of relations between the two countries, it was clear that this negotiation had taken place virtually in complete secrecy. Similarly, instances of track-two or unofficial diplomacy, such as the negotiations in Oslo, Norway, that resulted in the Oslo Accords of 1993 between Israel and the PLO (discussed in detail in chapter 5), usually require that completely private negotiations take place, lest the parties be subjected to insurmountable internal pressures from extreme elements within their societies.

Other negotiations, however, are very public in nature. For example, the various negotiations on the environment and climate change or the negotiations on the Law of the Sea or the Universal Declaration of Human Rights take place squarely in public view. While this does not mean that private negotiations do not take place among delegates in the corridors of the main halls, the venue is largely public, with interested parties watching.

Sometimes the line between private and public is intentionally crossed when parties, in an effort to scuttle the negotiations, leak details that, by themselves, could be seen back home as threatening to one or more of the parties. In other instances, the parties may use selective public leaks from what is largely a private negotiation in order to test the waters or to otherwise put some public pressure on the other parties in the negotiation. The more public a negotiation becomes, the less it resembles a negotiation and the more it takes on aspects of a public meeting, like the UN General Assembly, where speeches intended for domestic consumption, or for the benefit of alliance partners, often replace hard bargaining. But depending upon the nature of the issue, and how much is already known, it may not always be possible or even desirable to keep the negotiations under wraps.

Outcome

Negotiations also differ according to whether or not agreements are mandatory. Some negotiations, particularly those that take place under crisis conditions, require some sort of agreement for the crisis to end. This does not mean that the crisis will be resolved quickly, even if negotiations are ongoing. Consider, for example, the year-long negotiation to resolve the Iran hostage crisis of 1979–1981 or the two-year negotiation that led to the end of the Vietnam War in 1973–1975. But in these and other similar instances, there was a perception by both actors (although perhaps not held with equal strength) that an agreement had to emerge no matter how long it took.

Many other international negotiations take place in an atmosphere in which the actors have the option of walking away—perhaps with an understanding to meet again at a set time, perhaps not—and in which the only consequence is delay and possibly failure. In a noncrisis atmosphere, while the stakes may be high for some or all of the actors, the lack of urgency dampens the need to reach agreements quickly. So, for example, the Law of the Sea treaty took fourteen years to negotiate, the SALT agreements ten years, the Uruguay Round seven and a half years, and the Kyoto agreement five years (starting with Rio).

There are also instances where what began as a negotiation that did not require an agreement is transformed into one that does because of a sudden change in circumstances. The prospect of a transfer in the national leadership of one of the parties to the negotiation may transform what was a leisurely approach to a negotiation into one that suddenly takes on some urgency and may even become a crisis for the actors. The underground nuclear tests conducted first by India and immediately thereafter by Pakistan in the spring of 1998 had the effect of adding urgency to the virtually nonexistent negotiations between the two countries over the status of Kashmir and other outstanding issues. At the extreme, the Soviet threat to move tactical nuclear weapons to the eastern Mediterranean during the 1973 Middle East War raised the stakes in that crisis to a new level and created an extreme sense of urgency among those involved in attempting to negotiate a cease-fire between Israel and Egypt.

As noted earlier, the actors may differ in terms of their respective need to reach an agreement in a timely manner or even over whether an agreement is necessary at all. The actor that needs the agreement more may find itself at a disadvantage in the negotiation since it may have to make significant concessions in order to attain its goals. The United States appeared to need an agreement to end its involvement in the Vietnam War with greater urgency than did North Vietnam, and so the North was able to extract concessions from its more powerful opponent. Under the threat of continued atomic bombing of the population centers on its mainland in World War II, the Japanese were compelled to make concessions involving some of the most central institutions of their culture, among them the status and authority of the emperor.

Ratification Issues

When actors operate under different ratification rules and expectations, negotiations can often fail, owing to incomplete understanding of the domestic constraints under which each party operates. Thus, it is important to know whether negotiation teams can reach a final and formal agreement or whether further decision-making bodies need to ratify the agreement. During the long series of talks between the United States and the USSR leading to the SALT agreements, it was clear that the actors differed substantially in terms of ratification requirements. Agreements reached by the American team, representing the president of the United States and therefore the executive branch, had to be ratified by Congress before they became official U.S. policy. By contrast, the Soviet negotiators had more authority to negotiate final agreements, subject to the approval of a small group of advisers appointed by the Soviet leadership. In this latter case, while approval was not automatic, it was far more predictable than it was for the U.S. negotiators on that same issue.

Perhaps the classic example of this phenomenon is Woodrow Wilson's dramatic failure to secure U.S. Senate ratification of the treaty establishing the League of Nations in 1920. He might have been able to win ratification if he had pushed for alterations in the league charter, especially in one article that seemed to imply that the League could force the United

States into war. Not only was the ratification defeat a significant embarrassment to Wilson and the U.S. negotiators, but the practical consequence of the absence of the United States from League of Nations deliberations was a serious impediment to the ability of that organization to perform its peacemaking functions. This failure ultimately contributed to the League's inability to act decisively as the storm clouds of war gathered over Europe in the late 1930s.

In a negotiation, such constraints can be exploited by an adversary, who might indicate that despite the "obvious" reasonableness of a particular formula for agreement, it would never survive the ratification process back home and hence needs to be modified. At the extreme, negotiators might threaten that were they to agree to a particular outcome, it would almost certainly mean the fall of their government, with the less attractive possibility of a group with an even harder negotiation stance coming to power. Clever manipulation of both public opinion and political coalitions back home can often strengthen the hand of the negotiators at the table. In the early 1990s, Israeli prime minister Rabin noted that while he was in favor of the return of the Golan Heights to the Syrians, such a position was a complete nonstarter insofar as the majority of the Israeli population was concerned and hence could not be considered as part of the complex negotiation then under way through various intermediaries.

A related issue has to do with how binding a negotiated agreement is on the actors concerned. Were the Oslo Accords of 1993, negotiated by persons close to the somewhat "dovish" Israeli Labour government of Yitzhak Rabin and Shimon Peres, binding on the more "hawkish" Likud government, which won the subsequent election under Benjamin Netanyahu? And how might the actors make adjustments to a negotiated agreement as circumstances change? Is Cuba forever bound by agreements negotiated by previous governments involving the leasing of Guantanamo Bay to the United States, especially in light of vastly changed circumstances in the last third of the twentieth century?

Suspicions about how binding particular agreements might be on one's adversary in a negotiation can have a serious impact on the types of agreements that may be reached. Not unlike the issue of ratification, these suspicions can lead to a minimalist approach to the negotiations, whereby an actor is willing to make only minor and nonrisky concessions, so that a possible later renunciation of the agreement by the other actor would have limited negative impact. Or consider the elaborate inspection and verification procedures built into the SALT agreements, designed to make sure that the actors continue to live up to their ends of the bargain. Various confidence-building measures designed to increase the level of trust between the actors may be built into an agreement. Lacking this trust, such provisions can at least make defection from a negotiated agreement costly for the defector in some tangible way.

Legacy

In the international system, it is generally the case that the actors in one negotiation will meet again across the negotiation table. In many instances, they may be dealing with an aspect of the same issue, as is the case with a violent outbreak during an ongoing, protracted conflict. For example, Israel and Syria negotiated—with U.S. mediation—a cease-fire agreement ending their 1973 war, but they have negotiated on other related issues over the years since then, including missile placement in the Beka'a Valley in Lebanon in 1986, the Lebanon War itself in 1989, and, most recently, the future status of the Golan Heights, again with U.S. mediation. In other instances, the actors may meet again over issues seemingly unrelated to the first negotiation. Consider, for example, the myriad issues that are the subjects of current negotiations between the United States and Russia, ranging from economics, security, and the environment to nuclear proliferation and Yugoslavia. Finally, actors may find themselves adversaries in one negotiation and allies in another—for example, the United States and Japan in the economic and security arenas, respectively.

In all such cases, the repetition in negotiations produces a legacy that carries over from one negotiation episode to the next. Thus, tactics that have been used in one instance will be remembered the next time around. If an actor has employed bluffing, or at least been suspected of its use in an earlier episode, it will be much more difficult for that actor to establish a credible bottom line

> **KEY TERM**
>
> **Legacy** A repetition in negotiations; a carryover from one negotiation episode to the next.

in a future negotiation episode, even if the issues have changed. Similarly, if an actor drove a particularly hard bargain earlier, perhaps to the point where the other party to the previous negotiation views the outcome as a serious defeat and even a loss of face, then aspects of that perception will carry over into a future round of negotiations, perhaps engendering a "never again" attitude on the part of the previously humiliated actor. At the very least, it can make the climate at the negotiation table extremely strained.

In the heat of a serious negotiation, it may not always be possible to keep the issue of repetition in mind. While it may be tempting to extract maximum concessions now, the prospect of facing a very hostile adversary in a future round is unappealing. Negotiating in a way that allows the other actor to emerge with some degree of self-respect is more likely to result in a positive atmosphere over the long term. In its study of crises in the twentieth century, the International Crisis Behavior Project found that 44 percent of all crises terminated in such a way that the same actors were again involved in a crisis within five years (Brecher and Wilkenfeld, 1997, 757). A more positive negotiation atmosphere, coupled perhaps with a win-win approach to the outcome, may mean that future issues arising between these actors will not need to be dealt with in a crisis environment. The harsh conditions imposed on Germany as a result of the negotiations ending World War I created a negative climate in which the seeds of Nazism and the Second World War were sown. On the other hand, despite exceedingly hard bargaining and brinkmanship, the Cuban Missile Crisis ended in such a way that the USSR avoided complete humiliation by being able to claim that it had extracted some concessions from the United States in the form of the removal of American missiles from Turkey.

Summary

Every international negotiation episode takes place in context. Two dimensions of this context are of particular importance: the international system setting, which provides a framework for negotiation, and the individual characteristics that mark each specific negotiation episode. At the system level, negotiations take place within one of many historical power configurations—on a continuum from unipolar to multipolar, indicating the way power is distributed among states at any point in time. The presence of a crisis, with the increased sense of threat and urgency it invokes, significantly impacts the reception of a particular negotiation opportunity and the dynamics of the ensuing talks. Another system-level factor that can help define a negotiation is the presence of third-party intervention—sometimes in the negative form of pressure or interference from outside the negotiation sphere, other times in a positive form, with a neutral party suggesting ways to move beyond the stalemate.

After establishing the climate in which the negotiations take place, the next step involves identification of the particular conditions of the negotiation episode in question, whether historical or current. To facilitate that step, a checklist of actor, issue, and process factors is presented. Together they determine the uniqueness of one negotiation as compared with another. This list of characteristics—from the number of actors involved to the extent to which ratification of an agreement is required at home—presents an image of a negotiation situation that may be quite simple and straightforward or multilayered and complex.

Chapters 3 and 4 will further develop a number of these negotiation factors in relation to the actors and issues that are central to most international negotiations; chapter 5 will describe their dynamic properties or strategic interactions. Chapter 6 will reflect on important trends in diplomatic negotiation.

Key Web Sites

Timeline of (U.S.) Diplomatic History: http://www.state.gov/www/ about_state/history/timeline.html

Mideast Peace Process (1): http://www.washingtonpost.com/wp-srv/inatl/longterm/me_peace/me_peace.htm

> (*Washington Post* Special Report. Other special reports are available at http://www.washingtonpost.com/wpsrv/inatl/longterm/special.htm.)

Mideast Peace Process (2): http://www.israel.org/peace/index.html

> (the Israeli perspective on the peace process: also available at http://www.mfa.gov.il/mfa/go.asp?MFAH000c0)

Mideast Peace Process (3): http://www.nytimes.com/library/world/mideast/mideast-peace-index.html (*New York Times* Issue in Depth)

Interactive Cuban Missile Crisis: http://hyperion.advanced.org/11046/

> (Be sure to visit the "Situation Room" to read the transcript and listen to audio clips from the ExComm meeting on October 18, 1962. Another clip from that same meeting is available from the John F. Kennedy Presidential Library at http://www.cs.umb.edu/jfklibrary/j101862.wav.)

Cold War International History Project, Woodrow Wilson Center: http://cwihp.si.edu/cwihplib.nsf?OpenDatabase&Start=1&Count=30&Expand=6

> (primary source documents from a number of cold war crises, along with explanatory notes and commentary)

The Uruguay Round: http://www.wto.org/wto/about/facts5.htm

> (overview of the Uruguay Round from the World Trade Organization (WTO); broader discussion of GATT rounds at http://www.wto.org/wto/about/facts4.htm)

Office of the High Representative in Bosnia and Hercegovina: http://www.ohr.int/

> (responsible for civilian implementation of Dayton Peace Accords)

UN Peacekeeping Operations: http://www.un.org/Depts/dpko/

> (UN peacekeepers "are dispatched by the Security Council to implement peace agreements, monitor cease-fires, patrol demilitarized zones, create buffer zones between opposing forces, and put fighting on hold while negotiators seek peaceful solutions to disputes.")

Group of 77: http://www.g77.org/

American Leaders Speak: Recordings from World War I and the 1920 Election, 1918–1920: http://memory.loc.gov/ammem/nforSubjects01.html

> (recorded statements made by American political leaders during the League of Nations debate; look under League of Nations in the subject index)

All of the above sites can be directly accessed from the website for this book: http://www.icons.umd.edu/negotiating/links.htm

3

The Players

The structure of negotiation in the international system is nuanced and complex. Diplomatic representatives of states, coalitions of states, and international organizations continue to play high-profile roles in the world of negotiation, as they have since the founding of the state system with the Peace of Westphalia treaty in 1648. Over the last several decades, however, they have had to make room for the many nongovernmental substitute states and anomalous actors that have crowded onto the world stage. These have risen to prominence largely in response to a multitude of newly internationalized issues such as the environment, health, human rights, democratization, narcotics, and crime.

The first part of this chapter looks at the various types of actors that impact international negotiations. Whereas diplomatic negotiation was once solely the domain of official state representatives, the trend now is toward what Kennan describes as "diplomacy without diplomats" (1997, 198). Instead of being professionals with years of resident, personal experience in specific regions or states, specialists these days are more likely to be issue experts. This shift can result in a new type of negotiation team, such as that assembled for the Kyoto climate talks, where government representatives sat right beside nongovernmental actors over the course of the negotiation. This trend has also given birth to a new kind of negotiator—the global diplomat—whose primary attachment is not to a nation-state, but rather to a transnational issue or cause. Such global diplomats are often part of a recognized group of experts on a specific issue, an epistemic community, defined by Haas (1992, 3) as a "network of professionals with recognized expertise and competence in a particu-

---

KEY TERM

Epistemic Community   A "network of professionals with recognized expertise and competence in a particular domain" (Haas 1992, 3).

KEY TERM

Track-Two Diplomacy Unofficial negotiations, wherein nationals not closely affiliated with the government are deliberately chosen as negotiators.

---

lar domain." These individuals and the nongovernmental groups they often represent have made significant inroads into the diplomatic negotiation arena during the 1990s. Their expertise is often requested at the fact-gathering stage of the multilateral negotiation process and then entered into the negotiation record to substantiate the nature of the problem under consideration.

The contemporary period has also seen a rise in the so-called track-two diplomacy or unofficial negotiations, wherein nationals not closely affiliated with governments are deliberately chosen as negotiators. At the Oslo negotiations between the Israelis and the Palestinians, for example, some of the representatives at initial meetings came from academic rather than governmental circles. Who negotiates is increasingly dependent on the issue at hand and the forum in which the dialogue takes place. Track-two forums, as well as single-issue, multilateral negotiations, tend to feature high levels of participation from various nontraditional actors.

The first part of this chapter looks at the range of traditional and nontraditional actors who are increasingly impacting diplomatic negotiations. The second half looks beyond these characterizations to identify what motivates actors to approach negotiations in the ways they do. While traditional assumptions of territorial allegiance are still valid for states, other sources of identity play increasingly important roles for state and nonstate actors alike, at both individual and group levels. Such factors as culture, ethnicity, and religion, as well as gender and status, can shed much light on negotiation dynamics.

Sovereign States as Negotiators

Representatives of states—governmental actors—are still the most significant players in the international negotiation arena, despite the proliferation of other involved players. Much routine diplomatic work is handled by professional diplomats, usually operating from embassies or through groupings of states, such as the UN. Their work is often augmented by that of top-level national leaders during times of crisis or intense media focus. And more and more in the international system, it is the case that important negotiation matters are being handled at the substate level, where burgeoning local and regional identities can rival those of nation-states.

The Diplomatic Corps

In the international system of states, negotiation has traditionally been the domain of diplomats formally assigned to serve their countries in foreign capitals. Diplomacy is a very old profession full of tradition and symbolism. To some, it is a professional fraternity (R. Cohen 1997, 20) with great emphasis placed on titles, hierarchy, and protocol. For example, when one country wishes to "slap" another for a perceived wrong, it works through the continuum of actions available to it—ranging from pulling some diplomatic personnel out of the host country, or downgrading its diplomatic mission there, to breaking off diplomatic relations. It is the great hope of international diplomacy that open or violent conflict can be avoided through this system of conventions, whereby responses ranging from trust to anger can be conveyed to other nations. The signals sent through diplomacy can be loud and clear, or they can be quietly symbolic. As part of its efforts to normalize relations with the Chinese in 1978, for example, the United States recognized the PRC as the "sole legal government of China" but added language stating that "within this context, the people of the United States will maintain cultural, commercial, and other unofficial relations with the people of Taiwan" (Bernstein 1995, 11). This seemingly innocuous statement was meant to signal Taiwan that it would continue to be afforded special diplomatic status, despite the return of an American ambassador to Beijing.

Much of the work of the diplomatic corps is routine. The overriding duty is to gauge political developments in the host country from a resident vantage point. The specific duties of the diplomat are many, including assessing, estimating, reassuring, and verifying incoming and outgoing information (Freeman 1997b, 121). The diplomat's mission is, most importantly, to try to preserve a peaceful balance in the relations between states and to lay the groundwork for negotiation possibilities in the event of tensions.

The mundane nature of the day-to-day functions of the diplomatic mission should not detract, however, from the very important role it needs to play in sensitive situations. Failure to interpret the changing political environment in a host country can be costly to overall foreign policy goals and strategy. In Tehran in 1979, for example, U.S. diplomats and embassy personnel found themselves at the center of a revolutionary storm when Iranian students took over their building and took them hostage. The occupation of the American Embassy represented a dramatic breach of widely accepted international diplomatic protocol, but it also highlighted a significant weakness in American-style country expertise. It turned out that the U.S. mission lacked contacts with persons outside of the royal court and the Western-educated elite. It also had very few officials who could speak Farsi at this very sensitive political time, which undoubtedly contributed to the misreading of events on the ground (Sick 1985, 77). The shah's abdication of his throne in early 1979 shocked the Carter administration. Caught off-guard, the United States did not respond well to the volatile situation. The intelligence and diplomatic fiasco reached its climax when American Embassy personnel were taken hostage. Negotiations for their release did not even take place until almost a year later, when Algerian officials were finally able to mediate a de-escalation of tensions by focusing some much-needed attention on the cultural issues inherent in the process.

Political Leaders

Much of the work that political leaders do in the negotiation realm takes place at a symbolic level. Major summits are usually the pinnacle of lower-level negotiations that have been ongoing, in some cases, for many months or even years. In certain cases, however, arduous negotiations are actually conducted from the top. As national security adviser and secretary of state in the Nixon and Ford administrations, Henry Kissinger became famous for his personal diplomacy (see box). During Kissinger's tenure as America's top diplomat, U.S. negotiations were more tightly controlled from the top than at perhaps any other time in recent history. Indeed, as more issues have risen in importance on the international agenda, this kind of control has been difficult to maintain for such powerful nations as the United States.

Jimmy Carter devoted a similar level of attention to personal diplomacy. His most impressive presidential legacy was his painstaking work to mediate the Arab–Israeli conflict, which led to a peace agreement between Egypt and Israel: the 1978 Camp David Accord. These negotiations gained their name from the time Carter and his Egyptian and Israeli counterparts, Anwar Sadat and Menachem Begin, spent at the U.S. presidential retreat. It was there that Carter guided the contentious negotiations by utilizing a so-called one-text procedure. Retaining control over the document that was to become the agreement, he personally negotiated with both leaders on important questions of wording and meaning, keeping the negotiations quite literally on the same page (Carter 1982, 396–397). The modern-day version of shuttle diplomacy has a troubleshooter or special envoy sent to work on difficult conflict situations. Richard Holbrooke in the Balkans and George Mitchell in Northern Ireland both spent several years trying to broker solutions that all the warring factions would accept.

In smaller countries whose foreign policy agendas are likewise more narrow in scope, it is not unusual for top political leaders to handle much of the diplomatic workload. For these states, foreign policy is more easily managed and the ties between domestic and international policy are often very close. For the Nordic nation of Norway, for example, the highly contentious issue of international restrictions on whaling goes to the very

Henry Kissinger: Personal Diplomat

As national security adviser to U.S. president Richard Nixon and secretary of state to U.S. president Gerald Ford, Henry Kissinger's place in diplomatic history as a gifted strategist and negotiator is secure. His style of personal diplomacy—shaping negotiations through sheer force of personality—was captured best through his tireless work in the Middle East following the October 1973 Arab–Israeli War.

Kissinger spent several years shuttling from capital to capital on bilateral negotiation missions, trying to establish a basis for broad, multilateral consensus on Egyptian–Israeli disengagement agreements. This personal style was the trademark of many more dealings as well, from Vietnam to the Soviet Union to China. Negotiating on behalf of a superpower, Kissinger found the corridors of power open to him. The approach was a very traditional one, as he negotiated one-on-one with the world's key leaders. His negotiation skills grew over time. Early on, at the laborious negotiations to end the Vietnam War, he was very focused on getting signatures on a peace agreement—any agreement, his critics charged. Later, negotiating with the Chinese on the "Shanghai Communiqué" in Beijing, he displayed more patience and developed the relationship-oriented style that would serve him so well in future difficult negotiation situations (R. Cohen 1997, 102).

In addition to the personal contacts cultivated on his many missions, Kissinger became a good listener and recognized certain cultural imperatives in his dealings with the Egyptians, Chinese, Russians, and so on. He developed a much more flexible means of dealing with important partners on various sticky issues. Critics of Kissinger and of his "great man" approach to international relations abound. But there is little doubt that his successes with personal diplomacy and its trademark shuttle diplomacy—trips back and forth between the principal parties—paved the way for a tradition now well established in U.S. diplomacy.

heart of the national economy and has become an issue of sovereignty. The Norwegian decision to defy the International Whaling Commission's (IWC) 1986 moratorium and resume commercial hunting came from the highest levels of national government. Norway even has a cabinet-level minister of fisheries, who works full time to arbitrate among different domestic constituency groups, as well as between Norway and the world community (Official Documentation and Information from Norway).

This type of high-level involvement can at times be advantageous to negotiations, speeding them up and bringing a higher sense of purpose and commitment. But it can also work against them. Brought to the brink of peace by the track-two-negotiated Oslo Accords, the Israelis and the

Palestinians reverted in the latter half of the 1990s to more traditional "top-down" negotiations. This change has resulted in intransigence since the outcome on every issue is now a matter of personal ego for the respective leaders of the two societies.

Groups of States

Individual states have varying levels of diplomatic leverage. Some are relatively powerless to affect a situation in which others far outweigh their clout. It is therefore to their benefit to join with others—either formally, through intergovernmental organizations or alliances, or temporarily, through coalitions—for the duration of the negotiations. Moreover, some problems require collective solutions—no state working alone can control the issue of ozone depletion, for example. Transboundary pollution respects neither state sovereignty nor national borders. For these reasons, it is not unusual for states to use organizational forums for negotiations. As part of these various interstate groupings, they attempt to pool their sovereignty in order to affect the outcome of the negotiations to the greatest extent possible. Certain groupings of sovereign states—NATO and the Organization of Economic Cooperation and Development (OECD), for example—very often act as single, independent actors in negotiations, at least after their internal member discussions have produced a consensus. They have the authority and credibility to speak on behalf of their member states in most cases. Hence, the media broadcast such pronouncements as "NATO is urging the Bosnian Serbs to return to the negotiation table to discuss the issue of ethnic Albanians in Kosovo" and "the OECD negotiated a voluntary code of conduct for multinational corporations."

As states have proliferated and their dealings with one another have become more complex, these official bodies have come to play very important roles in the diplomatic negotiation process. They not only function as clearinghouses for information, which can be of a highly technical nature, they also provide guidelines for international behavior. When well established, these guidelines become the norms and rules, or soft laws, that negotiators look to for an objective standard of fairness (discussed in detail in chapter 5).

Other intergovernmental actors also play more complex roles in negotiations. At the UN, the secretary-general, the Security Council, and the General Assembly—not to mention all of the various agencies—can play very different roles in the same negotiation episode. It is not unusual for them to play contrasting roles or to act as separate actors in the same situation. For example, in the Iraqi case discussed in chapter 1, the General Assembly voiced its displeasure with American plans to try to bomb Saddam Hussein into submission. In this body where every member state has an equal vote, less economically and militarily powerful countries often tend to side with the underdog in battles with great powers. At the Security Council, which has limited membership and stronger representation of the most powerful states in the system, a tougher stance was adopted toward Iraq in 1997–1998, although it still fell far short of what the United States and Britain had hoped for. Ultimately, it was the secretary-general himself who visited Iraq and mediated the crisis. Even as he went to Baghdad as a representative of the UN, Kofi Annan apparently carried with him explicit instructions from the United States on the acceptable parameters for the negotiations. It is difficult, therefore, to talk of a single UN role in this situation.

Similarly, the International Monetary Fund (IMF) has been a central figure in economic negotiations around the world, especially in trying to combat monetary crises in Russia, eastern Europe, Latin America, and Asia during the late 1990s. The IMF is generally thought of as an independent actor—requiring austerity measures for states in economic crisis in exchange for monetary relief—but it is actually an intermediary between the "will of the majority of its membership" and the individual member states that seek its financial help (Driscoll 1997). Its board of governors has been given the latitude to make decisions about payment policies, but it is clear that because of the fund's membership quota system—based on the amount of money each member contributes upon joining—the United States, Germany, Japan, Britain, and France have a disproportionate amount of power within the organization. In reality, the IMF does not act independently of sovereign states in the international system; rather, it is supposed to act to represent their best interests—a sort of commissioner of baseball for the world of international finance. It is essential to the effectiveness of the IMF, however, that member states be able to appear unrelated to the organization when it must play the role of the "heavy" in difficult negotiations.

The notion of pooled sovereignty also has a negative side. At times, states lament the erosion of their sovereignty by international governmental organizations. Led by the EU, there is also some movement toward supranationalism or extraterritorial allegiance within some institutions. In practice, this means that individual states are not always able to opt out of decisions with which they do not agree (Taylor 1984, 3). Debate still rages in Europe over whether the powerful EU Commission is a beneficial negotiation channel for its member states or whether it has effectively neutered them in certain arenas, most notably on monetary issues. Indeed, complaints that European foreign policies have been "EC-ized" (Ferguson and Mansbach 1996, 32) and that North Americans have lost control of their labor markets through NAFTA are commonly heard refrains as supranationalism makes inroads in several regions of the world.

Substates

Regionalism at the substate level is another noticeable trend that has resulted in some erosion of central governmental control over foreign policy. Numerous manifestations of this phenomenon—what one analyst

KEY TERM

Cross-Frontier Regional Organizations
Manifestations of regionalism at the substate level; can result in erosion of the central governmental authority over foreign policy.

called cross-frontier regional organizations—occur in different areas of the world (Langhorne 1997, 7). In the United States, for example, individual states have developed close ties of their own to regions that are of special geographic and ethnic importance to them—California to East Asia and Mexico, and Florida to the Caribbean and South America. California has its own Office of California–Mexico Affairs, along with many foreign trade offices in Africa, Asia, and Europe. The state of Florida has been influential in negotiations over the establishment of the Free Trade Area of the Americas (FTAA), going so far as to release position papers that urge not only the government of the United States but also those of South American countries to adopt certain stances (Ponce 1997).

In the post–cold war era, many substate actors have behaved in a manner independent of their national leadership to establish strong cross-border ties. Various *länder* (states) in Germany were the first to try to reestablish a long-dormant "Baltic identity." They linked themselves to Russian Baltic port cities and to the newly independent states of Estonia, Latvia, and Lithuania, as well as the Nordic states. The Special Economic Zones started in Canton Province, China, have served a similar purpose. Explicitly linking Canton to neighboring Macau and Hong Kong provided the Chinese with an important test case of the "one country, two systems" policy that defines their post-1998 relationship with Hong Kong. The linkage has also led to an integrated Pearl River Delta region, where economic complementarities and competition offer the Chinese exposure to the complex workings of free-market economies. There have also been substantive gains in international reach for many cities. Some are embarking to a greater degree on the formulation of their own diplomacy. Lyon, the center of France's Rhone-Alpes region, has its own embassies in Germany, Switzerland, and Italy (Matthews 1997, 62). In the United States, New York mayor Rudolph Giuliani caused a diplomatic incident in 1995 when he sent representatives to Lincoln Center to escort PLO chairman Yasir Arafat out of the theater. Giuliani claimed he would not "serve as a gracious host to anyone who had engaged in terrorism" (Reuters and Associated Press 1995). But the incident shocked the Clinton White House, which feared it would upset the sensitive Middle East peace negotiations under way in Madrid at the time.

Some observers now refer to regional and substate identities—some newly formed, some rediscovered—as the third level of international policy-making (Jeffrey 1997, 1). Traditionally confined to cultural negotiations only, regional entities have begun to negotiate in policy areas previously reserved for national governments, including security and economics. The proliferation of interstate groupings and the growth in new diplomatic actors at the substate level have complicated the formulation of negotiation strategies and the conduct of negotiations for state actors. The simultaneous but contradictory forces of integration and devolution encroach on state sovereignty from different directions, complicating the calculus of national interest so important to the negotiation process.

Nongovernmental Actors in Negotiation

Increasingly, negotiation situations feature actors that are neither sovereign states nor reliant on those states for membership and direction. This book considers various nongovernmental actors who exert significant impact on diplomatic negotiations in the state arena. Many international business textbooks look at yet another phenomenon: episodes in which private entities negotiate transnationally with other private parties. Although negotiations in that private arena can impact or spill over into the state realm—for example, negotiations between U.S. and Japanese auto makers—it is for the most part outside the purview of this text.

It has been hypothesized that nongovernmental actors tend to gain more prominence in policy areas where there has been significant state failure (Skocpol 1988, 293). This does ring true for a variety of endeavors, such as the pursuit of private economic interest, the protection of the environment, and the protection of individual and group rights. A broad array of nongovernmental actors work in the international arena, performing a variety of functions. Some are stand-ins for states; others work to influence the diplomatic agendas of states. The following section looks at these types of nongovernmental actors and the important roles they play in the contemporary international arena.

Substitute States

A number of entities serve as stand-ins for nation-states in the negotiation arena, in essence acting as substitute states. Although very different in legitimacy and scope, these entities perform similar negotiation functions, acting in the place of national govern-

> **KEY TERM**
>
> **Substitute States** Entities that replace or rival the authority of the nation-state and its diplomatic capacity.

ments. The need for articulation and representation of the economic, security, and political interests of such stateless groups as the Palestinians and the Kurds, for example, led to the formation of the rebel groups known as the PLO and the Kurdish Worker's Party (PKK). In Sierra Leone and some other West African countries, the penetration of the state system by foreign firms and global business interests is seen by some observers as so advanced that it has created new, elite networks with more power than national governments (Reno 1996). In Freetown, for example, an Iranian-backed Palestinian group was allowed to establish an *embassy* in return for a promise of private access to Iranian oil on easy credit terms. The establishment of a shadow state—a virtual buyout of the state—puts a price on legitimacy and establishes the values of the free market as superior to those of sovereignty and territoriality.

In some other countries, private interests are so highly structured that they rival the central state for authority over international matters, including negotiations. In Japan, private business interests were for a long time so well organized and exerted so extensive a control on state policy that some observers wryly renamed the country "Japan, Inc." In other societies, such as El Salvador in Central America, vast family networks tend to represent subregional economic interests.

Other forces, many of which lack political legitimacy and authority, challenge state sovereignty. Currency speculators have not yet taken a seat at the negotiation table; nonetheless, they exercise great importance in the international financial market. Powerless to stop his country's financial crash in 1997, Malaysian prime minister Mahathir Mohammad publicly blamed international currency speculators for Asia's woes, lamenting the degree to which this amorphous group can erode state sovereignty. Likewise, in the South American country of Colombia, illegal drug cartels conduct an estimated $5 billion per year in business, accounting for almost 10 percent of its gross domestic product. This degree of wealth means tremendous influence for the cartels in almost every aspect of Colombian political and social life.

Various transnational forces and movements can also rival the state in legitimacy and authority, ultimately affecting negotiations on a variety of issues. The so-called Islamic movement is one such example. Political Islam actually has many different faces and rarely speaks with one voice, but it did find a common position during the height of the Bosnian conflict, when there was widespread, open support for the arming of the Bosnian Muslims in their struggle against the Serbs. Some Muslim groups even managed to funnel weapons to them.

Nongovernmental Organizations (NGOs)

A vast number of NGOs exert an impact in the diplomatic negotiation arena. In environmental politics, their influence has greatly contributed to the 100 percent growth in the number of multilateral treaties signed over roughly the last two decades (Matthews 1997, 59). In the area of human rights, the NGO Amnesty International has formed a vast cross-border network of citizen groups that, through write-in campaigns and other tactics, routinely exert pressure on states that violate human rights. Not only does it act as an international lobbyist in this area, but Amnesty International also provides expert witnesses to shed light on certain situations for which little information is otherwise available to states.

In the past, there has been a tendency for states to dismiss many such actors as protest groups. The influence attained by the environmental NGO Greenpeace at the international level and as an electoral presence in many individual countries, however, probably did more than any other

The New Negotiators: Global Diplomats

As certain issues have ascended to global status in the international arena, a new kind of negotiation actor has grown in importance. On the individual level, this is the international civil servant working on issues related to the environment, human rights, population, development, and other social concerns, often as part of an authoritative, epistemic community of experts. The allegiance of this global diplomat is to an area of transnational concern. The work arena is the vast NGO network.

Rather than the personal power that serves as the main negotiating tool of the Henry Kissingers of the world, the global diplomat uses scientific evidence or other in-depth knowledge of the issue area to impact negotiations. Personal anonymity is the unspoken rule. Global diplomats spur states on to negotiate in areas that are not always high on their national agendas. They do this by creating frameworks and forums into which state actors can easily be integrated. These NGO networks are adept at finding creative ways to influence negotiations. The Climate Action Network (CAN) produced the influential *ECO* newsletter in Kyoto, which reportedly became a "must read" for all participants onsite and was also disseminated over the Internet to interested observers outside of Japan. CAN is an umbrella group of over 250 NGOs or citizen-based organizations that work on strategies for combating climate change. It has eight regional launching points: Africa, South Asia, Southeast Asia, Latin America, central and eastern Europe, Europe, the United Kingdom, and the United States. One of its main functions is to organize the tremendous amount of information that exists on climate change. This means that CAN must stay on top of the huge amount of data that exist on the national, regional, and international dimensions of this issue. It also formulates policy positions, which it explains in position papers that it distributes. Finally, it serves as a channel for collaboration among NGOs working on this issue as they enter the policy arena. CAN is now considered a formidable player in negotiations on climate-related issues. It counts among its member organizations the transnational Greenpeace, Friends of the Earth, and World Wildlife Fund, as well as numerous national and regional environmental action groups.

Global diplomatic actors—whether individual scientists or activists, or vast networks of NGO—represent a new force in the international negotiation arena. Their ability to mobilize public opinion and political action is unprecedented and closely tied to the information revolution of the late twentieth century. Ted Turner's Cable News Network (CNN) and the Internet's World Wide Web represent potent tools in NGO campaigns to educate and organize people around the world in areas where governments have been slow to respond.

single factor to change this perception. Now NGOs often represent their issue-based constituencies at international negotiations or join with state delegations to bring their perspectives in approach and opinion. Their enhanced respectability and roles have led to the formation of an entirely new type of negotiation actor: the global diplomat.

Actor Dynamics

Many factors help determine how players will behave in negotiation situations. Subsequent chapters will discuss such major elements as issue intensity (stakes) and strategic decision making (moves). Each of these explanatory approaches is based, to some extent, on the assumption that states react similarly in certain situations. In contrast, the remainder of this chapter will consider the factors that differentiate actors' motivations from one another.

KEY TERM
"Othering" The politicization of cultural differences between negotiation parties.

The relationship of negotiators to identifiable rules of the game or international norms is an important reference point for this discussion, tempered by culture and identity. When such sources of meaning and understanding are in conflict, "othering" is often the result—the politicization of cultural differences between negotiation parties.

The Rules of the Game

Although a system in only a conceptual sense, there exists a prevailing international order, defined by such key principles as state sovereignty and territoriality. Critics lament this system's lack of punitive power and enforceable law, but great strides have been taken in the post–World War II period to create a set of norms that govern state behavior. Many of these concepts have been spawned by Western institutions—such as the Bretton Woods monetary system—and are therefore controversial for some non-Western states. For better or worse, however, these institutions have defined the rules of the game in the international system.

The relationship of actors to this system and its norms is an important factor in negotiation and has many different dimensions. At the broadest

KEY TERM
International Regimes Informal international institutions organized around "sets of mutual expectations" (Ruggie 1975).

level, it is necessary to establish whether the actors in the negotiation under examination are in good standing in the system. In other words, are they considered good neighbors? Evidence of positive standing includes active participation in international organizations, international regimes—informal institutions organized around "sets of mutual expectations" (Ruggie 1975, 570)—and other collective institutions. Negative indications involve nonparticipation in the defining institutions of the system and aggression against other states, including certain expansionist and irredentist policies designed to unilaterally extend national borders. At the extreme negative end are so-called rogue states, which deliberately reject prevailing norms in a broad array of areas—most notably security—and which often refuse negotiation as an option for conflict resolution.

However, between those predominantly Western states that define many of the rules of the game and those few who deride them are the majority of members of the international system. Many are classified as economically developing and politically democratizing. They are not readily welcomed into the many clubs: the Group of 7, the OECD, and that most exclusive of bodies, the acknowledged nuclear powers—all of which act to define the rules of the game. This leads to angry complaints about the existence of an international hierarchy and Western-contrived definitions of values. Indeed, one step down from generally accepted norms such as sovereignty is another layer that is highly controversial, including such value-laden areas as human rights. In defending its "one couple, one child" policy against criticism from Western states, for example, the Chinese government charges the West with cultural imperialism.

These kinds of fundamental disagreements about the norms of the system can hinder the negotiation channel at the very times it is most needed. Research shows that negotiation actors are more likely to negotiate successfully with states like them (Druckman and Broome 1991, 571). In other words, negotiation has a better chance when cultural misinterpretation is at a minimum. The next section on culture and identity will explore how different appearances, assumptions, languages, roles, and values can affect the course of negotiations.

Culture and Identity

Diplomacy is not just about bargaining. There is a human dimension to the negotiation game that should not be ignored. The process of reaching negotiated settlements to problems relies upon the willingness of all actors involved to sit down together and look for common solutions. Peaceful coexistence in the system of states rests upon a notion of mutual recognition. Often, when negotiation has proven futile over a long period of time, it is likely that diplomatic recognition and, indeed, basic group recognition did not exist. This has been true, to various degrees, of the Arab–Israeli conflict for over fifty years. Limited progress in this area has only been achieved since Israel received recognition from some of the surrounding Arab states and since the Palestinians were accorded official status as a party to the conflict.

Are nations' cultures really so different from one another? The main reference points are the same across most lands—family, community, authority, and religion—but Lewis asserts in *When Cultures Collide* that these concepts are viewed from different perspectives (1996, 2). It is this different angle of vision that leads to culturally grounded misunderstandings in international relations (see Barber 1995).

In the negotiation realm, culture is operationalized mainly through different styles of communication. Different verbal and nonverbal patterns of expression, ways of organizing information, and relationships to time and space are major elements. Differences along these dimensions can translate into discordant definitions of such concepts as timetable, fairness, and closure. There are often problems, as well, with very specific notions such as reciprocity, which many Western negotiators consider to be crucial to successful negotiation processes. This idea—that both sides should make equal concessions as they move toward agreement—places a high premium on compromise. Cross-cultural analysis shows us, however, that compromise is not valued equally—or even at all—in some cultures. It can, in fact, connote a bad agreement—one that neither side really wanted, thereby suggesting a lose-lose outcome (R. Cohen 1997). There is also much cultural misunderstanding surrounding the notion of issue discreteness in negotiations. Some states focus on the larger relationships they have with their negotiation partners when they sit down to negotiate, ensuring the establishment of a broad context for the talks. Other states do not see the utility of this approach and prefer to devote attention only to the issue at hand. The misunderstanding and even bickering that ensue can stall negotiations before they have had even a chance of success. Many misunderstandings and incompatibilities that occur at the negotiation table are due to these different interpretations of key reference points (R. Cohen 1997). Skillful negotiators can often move around them by having an understanding of their counterparts' cultures. However, even if negotiators successfully maneuver through this labyrinth, they must then manage the challenge that comes from competing identities, from the national level on down.

Where the interests of negotiation players are very different or even competing, elements of individual and group identity can become dangerously politicized. Identity is about the self in relation to others. Since resources are scarce the world over, anything that differentiates people from one another—including ethnicity, gender, language, race, and religion—can become a potential source of conflict. Identities are easily perceived as competing, giving rise to "us versus them" or "othering" scenarios: Jews and Arabs, men and women, French and English, and whites and blacks.

Many contentious negotiation situations involve competing identity groups. Moving beyond obvious differences to engage in a joint process such as negotiation may not come easily. When racial, ethnic, and religious differences are involved, contrasting appearances, roles, and rituals often block the abilities of negotiators and the broader societies they represent to find what they share—some common values in addition to their competing ones. In the old city of Jerusalem at the Temple Mount, for example, Jews revere the Wailing Wall and Muslims the Dome of the Rock.

Women and International Negotiation

Underrepresented in national leadership roles, women have long wielded more influence in local politics. With emphasis placed on health, peace, nutrition, and environmentally safe and technologically appropriate development strategies, women have argued strenuously for greater state and international accountability to ordinary citizens. As the relative power of NGOs has grown over the past ten to fifteen years, so has the global influence of women. Many have assumed leadership positions in these organizations and in the influential networks of organizations working on various humanitarian issues. Their work is focused primarily on agenda setting in the international arena—trying to bring peace, ecology, and other similar concerns to the forefront of national agendas.

The many women's groups active in the international arena—such as Women in Northern Ireland, Women for Life on Earth, Oxford Mothers for Nuclear Disarmament, and many hundreds more (Peterson and Runyan 1993, 126)—are working to change perceptions of issues and goals. They are also working to persuade states to embrace different strategies in their struggles with one another. Women's groups' struggle against war has been central for many decades. More recently, work on the disproportionate burden that economic sanctions place on the women of targeted societies has appeared. A recent UN-funded study found that sanctions against Iraq in the areas of health, sanitation, illness, and food shortages overwhelmingly affect its women, given their responsibilities for rearing children and maintaining households (Buck, Gallant, and Nossal 1998, 81).

Their dual presence on this site makes it one of the holiest in the world to these ethnic groups. But because they are unable to settle their competing claims to the land upon which the site is found, the Temple Mount has been the site of bloody confrontations between followers of the two faiths.

It is also the case with identity politics that the international system sometimes acts as more of a reference point for action than does the nation-state. Such is the case with "women's issues" in international relations. Here, gender identification cuts across national lines as women's interests coalesce around certain issues that they feel disproportionately affect them worldwide.

"Othering"

Deep cultural misunderstandings or disconnections can impede the mutual understanding that is so important to negotiation; so, too, can competing identities, where resources and legitimacy are deemed scarce. But the most dangerous obstacle to meaningful negotiation is the invocation of these differences to demonize the "other," thereby putting cooperation out of reach.

Why do culture and identity matter in negotiations? After all, it is the *problem* between two or more actors that is supposed to be the focus, not the actors themselves. However, research on negotiation patterns reveals a predisposition to negotiate with and negotiate successfully with those who are most like oneself, as opposed to those designated as the "other." Huntington (1993, 35) talked about this phenomenon in terms of "kin-country syndrome" replacing political ideology as the main determinant of cooperation. It does seem logical that where there are commonalities in, for example, history and language, there would be a greater basis for trust and understanding. The successful contemporary relationship between the United States and Britain would seem to bear this out, even though the shared history involves a violent revolution. But what of other pairs, such as India and Pakistan, Ethiopia and Eritrea, Cambodia and Vietnam, and Greece and Turkey? In these relationships, various commonalities are overridden by highly charged sources of differentiation (religious, ethnic, territorial) that have, for the most part, made meaningful negotiation dialogue impossible.

The key point here is that culture and identity are dynamic, interactive forces. When they are not invoked and "othering" is not a factor, then the negotiation relationship is usually based on the issues at hand. This was true of the Americans and the Soviets during the detente period of the cold war during the 1970s, after the initial hysteria over competing ideologies had died down and before Ronald Reagan ushered in a new, highly confrontational era of cultural "othering" with his use of the "evil empire" image.

Sometimes cultural differences are not understood and are instead an implicit factor defeating cooperation between parties. This has been true of the relationship between the United States and Japan, where little cross-cultural understanding has been achieved and disdain for each other's culture has often been professed instead. And then there are the situations where identification vis-à-vis the "other" is so intense that meaningful dialogue is effectively blocked. This has been true of the Greek and Turkish Cypriots, as well as the Israelis and the Palestinians. "Othering" can therefore be visualized as taking place along a kind of continuum from awareness of differences, but with no substantial impact of them on negotiations, to definition of one's own interests only in opposition to those of the other. The following three brief examples illustrate this point.

The Soviet–American Cold War Relationship: A Dangerous Trust

One of the lessons learned from the forty-five–year cold war between the United States and the Soviet Union is that even states with seemingly opposed values can successfully negotiate with one another. The explanation for this apparent inconsistency lies in the dynamic nature of culture and identity as forces in the international system. Cultural differences are not always invoked as reasons to avoid negotiation. Trust can be built regardless of these many differences when objectives are shared. The Americans and the Soviets shared a belief in the strategic doctrine of deterrence—the principle that their mutual willingness to destroy each other was a basis for cooperation. This mutual fear led to a shared value: the need for survival in the face of possible annihilation. This fear is what guided their behavior in such negotiations as SALT and the Strategic Arms Reduction Talks (START). It also led to placing great importance on open communication lines and active negotiation agendas. Indeed, out of their most dangerous confrontation—the Cuban Missile Crisis of 1962—came the hotline agreement that guaranteed a direct Teletype channel between the Kremlin and the White House. In the latter half of the twentieth century, the United States and the Soviet Union dominated international politics with their strategic showdown, but they also revealed an important negotiation principle: shared norms can emerge out of repeated (iterated) bargaining situations (Kratochwil 1984, 350). Negotiations can produce a laboratory-like setting in which enemies can become partners and cooperation, once learned, can be transformed from one arena to another when their common interest is great enough—for example, preventing nuclear war.

The American–Japanese Relationship: Trying to Understand the "Other"

The United States and Japan have a unique relationship, born of the role America played in reshaping Japanese politics after that country's defeat in World War II. The ensuing friendship was one of patron-client or, as some have characterized it, parent and child. Despite a strong political and military relationship between these two states over the past fifty years, growing problems since the early 1980s have threatened to derail it. Younger Japanese think it anachronistic to talk about deference to the United States, and they believe Tokyo must grow into its role as a world leader. Many Americans see unfairness in the relationship. They feel that the free trade that is supposed to underlie it is a sham and that Washington has long been taken advantage of by a Japan that welcomes American security protection but deceives the United States in economic matters.

The problems in this relationship are many. The most serious disputes have involved trade and monetary policies. They have centered on questions of market access, governmental protectionism, and currency valuation. The automobile sector has, over time, served as a microcosm of the troubles the two countries have had. CEOs of the American "Big Three" auto companies—Ford, General Motors, and Chrysler—complained bitterly in the 1980s that Japanese manufacturers—Honda, Toyota, Nissan, and others—were fully able to penetrate the U.S. market but resisted the reciprocation of this access. They accused the Japanese government of colluding with corporate conglomerates in its country to keep American cars and car parts out of its domestic market. The Japanese retorted that U.S.-manufactured products were often inferior and that American manufacturers had not even bothered to make their cars usable, let alone attractive, to Japanese consumers. As evidence, they pointed to a dearth of right-hand-drive American automobiles available in Japan.

All of this bickering did not stop the United States and Japan from negotiating. In fact, private-sector negotiations between companies such as Toyota and General Motors resulted in new hybrid, Japanese-designed U.S.-manufactured automobiles. But the relationship still hits trouble spots with great frequency, and the mutual recriminations are almost always the same: the U.S. government accuses its Japanese counterpart of not doing enough to make things right in the area of trade, to which Tokyo responds that the Americans have too narrow a view of capitalism. What is instructive about these exchanges is that the Americans frame the problems as economic and structural, while the Japanese respond by pointing to political factors. It has been up to academics and others in the social realm to point out that the major source of misunderstanding in this relationship is cultural (Oka 1992, 18 A).

Most objective analysts of U.S.–Japanese disputes agree that there is merit to the positions both sides take. The Japanese have benefited tremendously from their access to many sectors of the American economy. However, they do have a fundamentally different style of doing business. The producer, not the consumer, is revered in Japan. Moreover, networks of businesses work together closely to design, manufacture, and market. The resulting *keiretsu* system (loose conglomerates) does offend the tradition of antitrust sentiment in the free-trade lexicon, but it is an inherent part of the Japanese business culture, dating back to the pre–World War II *zaibatsu* (tight, family-controlled conglomerates). Across the board—from the relationship of business to government, to that of the state to its people—the Japanese emphasis on winning market shares as distinct from the U.S. emphasis on profit complicates this important international relationship. But as long as trust in the goodwill and good intentions of the "other" endure, the Americans and the Japanese will likely continue a successful negotiation partnership.

Catholics and Protestants in Northern Ireland: Mirror Imaging

The Anglo-Irish Treaty of 1921 granted independence to the twenty-six southern counties of Ireland—the Republic of Ireland—while preserving British governmental rule over Northern Ireland. It is in this northern area, often referred to as Ulster, that the minority Catholic population has been protesting British rule ever since. Discontent with what they deem as inequalities vis-à-vis the majority Protestant population, Catholics have used a variety of means, both violent and nonviolent, to try to affect the situation. Since 1969, Northern Ireland has been deeply impacted by the sectarian violence of paramilitary groups, most notably the IRA, but also the Ulster Volunteer Force (UVF) and others on the Protestant side. At times, IRA violence has been directed at the British through attacks on political figures and civilians in London. But the day-to-day conflict has been fought in the streets of Belfast, Derry, and the other cities of Northern Ireland, where the "troubles"—as the Irish characterize the bloody, protracted conflict—have resulted in over 3,200 deaths and over 20,000 injuries.

The conflict in Northern Ireland pits Republicans or nationalists (the Catholic minority that favors unification with the independent Republic of Ireland to the south) against Unionists or loyalists (the majority Protestants who favor continued union with the United Kingdom). Every aspect of competing group identities between the two sides has been politicized over the decades, with fault lines along class, national identity, and religious affiliation. Widespread segregation in housing and schools and allegations of discrimination in employment practices and the legal system provide the most obvious manifestations of "othering." Its more insidious outlets come through the symbolism of colors—green for the Republicans and orange for the Unionists, derogatory terms that children learn early on—*fenians* for the Catholics and *orangies* for the Protestants—and the various holidays and days of remembrance that each side regularly celebrates with emotionally charged parades (Robinson 1992; Jarman 1997).

Negotiations aimed at reconciliation of the many parties to this conflict (the Republicans and the Unionists are both split into various groups,

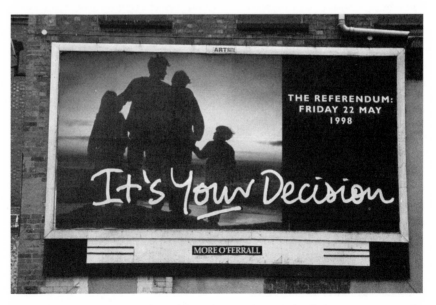

Billboard suggesting a brighter future for Northern Ireland if voters approve the Good Friday Peace Amendment, 1998. <http://cain.ulst.ac.uk>

and the United Kingdom and Irish Republic are central actors as well) failed to make any substantive progress until the 1997–1998 "All-Party Talks." These talks came about as a direct result of the extreme frustration that all sides felt when the paramilitary cease-fires of 1994 broke down in early 1996. The IRA resumed violence at that time, citing a lack of good faith on the part of then-British prime minister John Major. This perception of British intransigence was reinforced by then-prime minister of the Republic of Ireland, John Bruton, who stated, "Britain has [shown] less courage, generosity and decisiveness since the paramilitary cease-fires last year than [have] many people in Ireland" (Brams and Togman 1998, 35). Not long afterward, the Unionist cease-fire collapsed as well, and it was widely feared that the peace process had reached a dead end.

Several factors helped move the negotiations out of gridlock and back on track in 1997. One was the May election of Tony Blair as prime minister of Britain. Like his predecessor Major, Blair insisted that the IRA cease-fire be reinstated before peace negotiations could resume. However, he followed the lead of International Commission chairman George Mitchell (a former U.S. senator) in recognizing that IRA willingness to repeat the cease-fire move would not be likely unless the British promised to reciprocate quickly this time around. To this end, three weeks after his election, Blair went to Belfast to promise that if the Republican groups would take a conciliatory stance, "I will not be slow in my response" (Brams and Togman 1998, 37). Indeed, he did much to move the process forward by agreeing to Mitchell's proposal that the thorny issue of paramilitary disarmament be handled at the peace talks, rather than as a precursor to them. This promise of reciprocity and the personal attention and energy that Blair devoted to the situation moved all the parties forward once again. With cease-fires back in place and the parties finally at the negotiation table, Mitchell imposed a deadline of April 9, 1998, on the talks.

One day after the deadline, at Stormont Castle in Belfast, an announcement was made that an agreement had been reached. Dubbed the Good Friday Agreement, it outlined proposals for a Northern Ireland Assembly, political structures connecting the north and south of Ireland, new human rights legislation, normalization of security forces and policing practices, and a planned decommissioning of all paramilitary groups within two years after the endorsement of the agreement (Ingraham 1999, 11). In the first "all-Ireland" vote in the contemporary period, the Agreement was approved in joint referenda in Northern Ireland and the Republic of Ireland on May 22, 1998. In the north, nearly 97 percent of Catholics voted yes in support of the agreement, along with 51 to 53 percent of Protestants. Although there have been challenges to the will of the Irish people to stay with the agreement (most notably the IRA splinter-group bombing of civilians in Omagh, Northern Ireland, in August 1998), the referendum illustrates a crucial point about cultural conflicts and negotiations to end them: it is not enough for political leaders to sign on to peace agreements. When conflicts are so entrenched at the societal and cultural levels, it is ultimately the people who must decide to reconcile, take steps toward trust, and choose the path of negotiated peace over sectarian violence and hatred.

Summary

The diplomatic landscape has changed from the days of Henry Kissinger's personal diplomacy, and it continues to change—resulting from the diffusion of power from centralized, national governments to superstates, substates, shadow states, and a host of other related entities that have begun to practice their own foreign policies.

NGOs, the global diplomats who work from within them, and the vast networks they often form around issues such as health, the environment, and human rights can now mobilize tremendous power. The information revolution has brought with it a greater understanding of global problems and avenues of action for those experts and activists who work to coordinate international and transnational efforts in these areas.

The proliferation of issues on the proverbial negotiation table and the actors that bring them there have transformed the negotiation landscape. Identity politics has found its way into diplomacy, bringing new attention to old notions like peace, now very much a gender issue. The impact of women's groups on the international agendas of states is just one of the many influences on the changing rules of the game in the international negotiation arena.

Yet, despite these many dynamic elements, cultural "othering"—the villainization of the adversary—still blocks progress in many conflict situations. Despite what the Henry Kissingers of the world believed, negotiations and negotiated agreements are always extremely tenuous when they come from the top down. Reconciliation, it seems, must be accepted by those down below.

Key Web Sites

Foreign Service Journal: http://www.afsa.org/fsj/index.html
 (a view of American foreign policy from a diplomat's perspective)
Interview with Henry Kissinger for CNN's "Cold War" series: http://www.seas.gwu.edu/nsarchive/coldwar/interviews/epi sode-16/kissinger1.html
 (discusses rapprochement with China and SALT)
NATO: http://www.nato.int
California Trade and Commerce Agency: http://commerce.ca.gov/international/
 (highlights the work of this state governmental agency to increase international trade)

Amnesty International: http://www.amnesty.org/
Greenpeace: http://www.greenpeace.org/
NGOs and the UN: http://www.igc.org/globalpolicy/ngos/
    (information about and analysis of the role of NGOs in global
    policy making)
ECO: http://www.igc.apc.org/climate/Eco.html
    (The newsletter of CAN published at the UN climate talks in
    Kyoto)
Overview of Conflict in Northern Ireland: http://www.washington-
    post.com/wp-srv/inatl/longterm/nireland/n_ireland.htm
    (*Washington Post* Special Report)
Conflict Archive on the Internet (CAIN): http://cain.ulst.ac.uk/
    (Web service housed at the University of Ulster providing infor-
    mation about the "troubles" in Northern Ireland)

*All of the above sites can be directly accessed from the website for this book:
http://www.icons.umd.edu/negotiating/links.htm*

4

The Stakes

The UNSCOM crisis negotiations and the Kyoto environmental negotiations have been used throughout this book to highlight many
important dimensions of the negotiation process. They can also
illustrate the stakes for negotiators or, using the term that will be developed throughout this chapter, the *importance* of a negotiation issue to the
actors involved. The crisis in Iraq represents an example of what has traditionally been termed a high politics issue, with a focus on arms control
and other military–security concerns of the involved states. In contrast,
the concern with climate change in the Kyoto negotiations presents what
has traditionally been viewed as a low politics issue—of less urgency to
states and of lesser salience than a military–security matter. The aim of
this chapter is to illustrate how the issues involved in particular negotiations shape the negotiations themselves. This discussion focuses on what
gets discussed in international negotiations and how the issues determine
which actors get involved, the dynamics among the issues, and the types
of outcomes that result from the negotiation process. The chapter begins
with an examination of the traditional way issues have been viewed—the
high politics versus low politics dichotomy—and then moves on to a more
complex framework, shaped around the concept of issue salience.

The Traditional Issue Framework

The traditional way to think about issues in international relations is to classify them as high politics or low politics. Such classification frameworks are

admittedly limited since they cannot deal effectively with extremely complex or fluid situations; however, they represent a useful starting point for organizing the analysis of a given event or problem. As explained below, one of the reasons these terms have been used is that high politics issues are traditionally thought to exhibit larger degrees of participation on the part of top-level officials, thus accounting for their higher profiles. Low politics issues, in contrast, have traditionally been viewed as the domains of lower-level governmental officials. The following sections lay out in more detail the actors and issues associated with each domain of international activity.

High Politics

High politics issues have traditionally been seen as ones that threaten the survival of the state and thus demand the attention of its highest officials (Mansbach 1997). For example, in the United States during the cold war period, military–security issues around the globe consistently required the attention of the president and other high-level officials. In the post–cold war international system, however, military–security challenges are reappearing in many different forms and sometimes in unexpected places. U.S. secretary of state Madeleine Albright captured this new reality in comments she made after visiting the bombed American embassies in Kenya and Tanzania in August 1998. "It's like being in a war," she commented after the United States struck back at suspected terrorist installations in Afghanistan and Sudan. "I think we are embarked on a venture in which we have to deal over the long run with what is a very serious threat to our way of life" (Shenon 1998, 5).

Low Politics

If high politics issues have traditionally monopolized the attention of high-level officials in the foreign policy and negotiation arenas, then low politics issues—such as the environment, economic development, foreign aid, and health—have usually been perceived as the purview of lower-level career officials often buried deep within faceless bureaucracies. Negotiations over the disbursement of foreign aid, for example, are routinely conducted and overseen by legislative committees or special departments within governments. In humanitarian crises, as opposed to military–security ones, the dialogue about a proper response is often managed by international development agencies—for example, the U.S. Agency for International Development (AID) or the Swedish International Development Agency (SIDA)—and by NGOs such as the International Red Cross.

Returning to Mansbach's definition, then, because low politics issues are ones that are not perceived as threatening to the survival of the state, they are not viewed in the same light. In the past, this has meant that high-level decision makers are not usually involved in negotiations dealing with these issues. The lower-level officials who manage them are much less likely to receive significant public attention or media scrutiny during their negotiations on these matters. Even when invoking these differences, however, it is not always so easy to distinguish high politics from low, as the following sections will explain.

New Approaches to Issues

There have long been objections to the high/low politics framework described above, in part because it is an outgrowth of state-centered models of international relations and does not adequately describe the variety of forces present in the international system. The usefulness of the distinction began to undergo serious questioning as early as the 1960s, when interdependence among the main units in the system—the nation-states— began to increase greatly as a result of the growth of world trade and finance, developments in transportation, and the rapid pace of change in communications. This interdependence led to the globalization of many once local activities, such as those related to the environment. The impact of individual states' decisions on environmental action was now clearly seen as important to neighbors near and sometimes even far away. Visible linkage of high to low politics issues was also apparent during this time, with the Americans, Soviets, and others using foreign aid disbursement as a tool of foreign policy. High correlations, for example, were found between anti-Soviet sentiment and receipt of American foreign aid monies (Hook 1995). It was also clear that strategic concerns motivated the aid policies others adopted, including Japan, France, and Sweden.

It is important to understand that these so-called low politics issues have always been crucial to the majority of people around the world. From natural environmental disasters that have long disproportionately affected the Southern Hemisphere to the HIV–AIDS epidemic now threatening to spin out of control in parts of Africa and Asia, social issues have increasingly become political issues. Moreover, it is important to explore to what extent average citizens agree with their leaders about what constitutes high politics as opposed to low. This point is well illustrated in figure 4.1, which displays public opinion on U.S. government spending on the environment and military defense over time. As this figure shows, from 1973 to 1998, a significant portion of the American public has consistently viewed spending on the environment as too low and defense spending as either about right or too high.

Public sentiments about policy priorities have been an important factor in moving problems once relegated to various bureaucracies to center stage in international negotiations, including cross-border environment, health, and narcotics issues. The high profile attained by the 1995 Beijing World Conference on Women and the eventual attention of the Clinton administration to the 1997 Kyoto global warming talks represent

Figure 4.1 U.S. Public Attitudes toward Environmental and Defense Spending

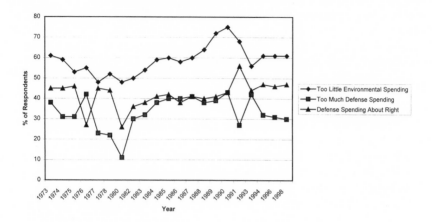

Source: National Opinion Research Center

instances of low politics issues coming to the forefront of world affairs and commanding the attention of high-level international policymakers in ways that run counter to traditional conceptions of issue categories.

On an institutional level, this gradual rise in importance of low politics issues has led to the negotiation of numerous international protocols and agreements, including, in the environmental area, the Law of the Sea, the Montreal Protocol on Ozone, and the Kyoto accords, among many others. Moreover, the increase in attention afforded formerly low politics issues has grown in the post–cold war international arena. Although military–security concerns have certainly not disappeared, the ability of many states to shift some of their attention to other issues has allowed more negotiations to focus on the broadening and deepening of economic ties among states. The EU movement toward monetary union and the creation of NAFTA provide two such examples. More than ever before, ordinary citizens and their political leaders cannot fail to note that successes and failures of others are related to their own economic well-being.

This rise in the importance of economic issues and the connections among economics, politics, and security were very evident in the series of events surrounding the Russian political crisis of the late summer of 1998. One journalistic account put the interrelationship and its impact in this understated way: "Wall Street opened in a sour mood Wednesday as the world's troubles caught up with U.S. investors after Russia effectively defaulted on its debt and the ruble plummeted" (Zang 1998). This "sour mood" ultimately translated into the largest single-day point loss in the history of the New York Stock Exchange and an extended period of significant market volatility throughout the major stock exchanges around the world. This kind of tumult presents new challenges in the negotiation arena as leaders ask themselves how they can collaboratively problem-solve in such situations.

Issue Salience in a Changing International System

One step that can move the discussion beyond the high politics/low politics approach is to introduce the concept of issue salience into the consideration of the impact of issues on the negotiation process (Boyer 1999b). Issue salience is the importance given to an issue by a particular actor or set of actors—the perceived stakes of the

KEY TERM
Issue Salience The importance a particular actor or set of actors gives to an issue—the perceived stakes.

issue. An example of an issue area that is highly salient for a broad cross section of political actors is international trade. The stakes perceived to be at risk—jobs, prosperity, and even environmental integrity—appeal to a wide array of actors and affect fundamental values for those actors.

Understanding variations in issue salience for the actors involved in international negotiations is an important step in the effort to build a more complex understanding of the ways issues affect negotiations. For example, even though environmental issues may be traditionally viewed as low politics, the stakes in cross-border environmental negotiations are very high for businesses that will confront rising energy costs, for groups that work to enhance environmental quality, and for those companies that stand to gain financially by providing technology for cleaner energy sources. Because the perceived stakes for these groups are so high, they will work very hard within their home political systems—and often internationally—to achieve their goals. This case makes it clear that the high/low approach overly simplifies the stakes for the interested parties by ignoring variations in salience. Focusing on salience gives more insight into why the same issue might at one point in time be very important but at other times of seemingly little consequence for the various stakeholders.

Sometimes, issues are highly salient for one group but less so for others. In U.S. politics, for example, Middle East peace negotiations are very important to members of the Arab-American and Jewish-American communities, but somewhat less so to others in the U.S. political system. In some cases, issues do not seem salient for many at the domestic political level at all. Efforts to get the Brazilian government to focus on the global impact of environmental issues—such as the destruction of the Amazon Rain Forest, for example—have not always been successful. With the exception of some "green" groups in Brazil, most domestic constituency groups have been much more concerned with improving economic growth and stability in that country than with environmental quality. The following section develops a framework based on issue salience as synonymous with perceived stakes.

To understand how issue salience can be so changeable for state actors, it is necessary to recognize the extent to which national interest has become complicated. Put simply, the determination of national interest is no longer an easy calculus for states to make, nor is it the only kind of interest that counts on the world stage. Increasingly, ethnic, corporate, transnational, and global interests—among many others—must be taken into account. The presence of such pressures at the domestic level is a particularly important factor in determining issue salience for state actors.

Although it is convenient to regard nation-states as monolithic entities, the reality of policy making is that many actors within countries vie for control of and influence over the outcomes of international negotiations. Members of legislatures who have opinions on international affairs that differ from those of the head of state, bureaucrats who work on specialized problems, and interest groups who champion certain causes often hold more narrow views on the desirability of certain policies. As a result, they work within the political system (and sometimes outside of it) to produce foreign policy decisions that will change the negotiations.

Of course, the fact that domestic constituencies participate in the negotiation game does not mean that they will all be happy with the outcome. At the conclusion of the Kyoto talks, many business groups were ultimately opposed to the signing of the Framework Convention on Climate Change because they did not want to have regulations imposed upon them that would raise production costs. Referring to U.S. negotiators, Bill O'Keefe, chairman of the pro-business Global Climate Coalition that opposed the Kyoto pact, argued, "We gave the store away. . . . We conceded everything. We got nothing. . . . There's no practical way we can reduce energy consumption in this country by over 30 percent in 12 years" (CNN Interactive 1997). Clearly, the fact that a company's home government signs an international agreement does not mean that everyone agrees with the position of the negotiators who—in theory at least—represented the national interest at the bargaining table.

One should also note that even if an issue is highly salient for domestic groups in one party to a negotiation, it is not necessarily very salient for those on the other side. The negotiations in the mid-1990s between Japan and the United States over the continuation of U.S. rights to maintain military bases on the Japanese island of Okinawa provide an excellent example of an issue that was highly salient for many Japanese citizens, particularly those living in the Okinawan prefecture, but received almost no attention in the United States, aside from that of some Pentagon administrators. When such situations occur, the flexibility and strategies of the various negotiators will be different even though they are discussing the exact same issue.

Because international negotiations have become so complex, it will be helpful to consider four sets of factors that influence issue salience: (1) the distribution of costs and benefits among domestic (substate) actors (which is essentially the controversy over the domestic stakes); (2) the commitment of key individuals and groups to the negotiation issue; (3) the urgency that the presence of a crisis situation adds; and (4) the level of media attention focused on the negotiations.

Controversial Domestic Stakes

Perceptions about the fairness of negotiated international agreements affect who gets involved in the negotiation process at the domestic level, as well as the salience of the issue for those actors. The degree to which any group feels that it is being unfairly burdened or that others are being unfairly rewarded will increase the intensity of that group's efforts to change policy course (Zimmerman 1973). Policies that impact society symmetrically are often less divisive and intense than policies that impact society asymmetrically, with some groups and individuals emerging as winners and others as losers. For instance, during the NAFTA negotiations (see NAFTA box later in chapter), Thomas Donahue (1991, 91), secretary treasurer of the AFL-CIO, wrote, "Among those who would suffer most from NAFTA are industrial workers in the United States. It would pave the way for tens of thousands of their jobs to be exported to Mexico, and it would bump hundreds of thousands down the economic ladder to underemployment and low wages." Fear of losing jobs to the Mexican market pushed narrow sectors of the American public and interest groups to argue against the signing of NAFTA by President Bush. Once it was signed, those same interest groups urged President Clinton to negotiate and sign the three side agreements to NAFTA and lobbied against approval of NAFTA by Congress, even though they ultimately lost their political battle. The vociferous opposition to NAFTA that labor unions put forth was motivated by their perception that the potentially high costs would be absorbed almost exclusively by American industrial workers.

Consideration of the perceived distribution of costs and benefits is also affected by short-term versus long-term calculations, as illustrated in the Kyoto case. Business interests looked at the short-term costs of meeting the emissions restrictions the Kyoto protocol imposed and focused on the impact this would have on production costs and, by extension, corporate profits in the short term. On the other hand, environmental groups looked at the long-term costs associated with global warming and tried to make the case for fast action—not an easy task—as they struggled against popular perceptions of a lack of immediacy. Thus, differences among the negotiation parties on short-term and long-term perspectives on who pays the costs and who derives the benefits may exacerbate conflict in the negotiation process.

Finally, it is also interesting to note in the Kyoto case that both business and environmental groups viewed the issue as highly salient, but for very different reasons: business because of Kyoto's potential negative impact on commercial competitiveness, and environmental groups because of the potential positive impact the accords might have on the control of global warming and its potentially catastrophic environmental effects. Perceptions of stakes create incentives for interested parties to work to sway public opinion on an issue.

Commitment to the Issue

Another factor that affects the salience of a negotiation issue is the level of commitment to the resolution of the problem by top leaders and other key domestic groups. High commitment can result from national pride, ethnic ties, deeply held political ideologies, perceived offenses, the personal interests and temperaments of the negotiators, and other causes. For example, the emotional legacy of anticommunist sentiment during the cold war, particularly among older Americans and western Europeans, translates now into merely lukewarm support for helping Russia out of its dire economic straits.

The impact of commitment on the ways issues are perceived in international negotiations can be both positive and negative. On the positive side, a personal stake on the part of negotiators may motivate them to work harder for an agreement, whether that agreement is ultimately a compromise or a perceived victory for their cause. King Hussein of Jordan had such a connection to the success of decades-long Arab–Israeli negotiations. Personal interventions and the ability of negotiators to capitalize on established relationships with other negotiators may mean the difference between success and failure. President Bush's tendency to take to the phone with other world leaders during times of crisis—his "Rolodex diplomacy"—added an individualized and extremely timely element to international negotiation during his presidency. These relationships paid off for him in 1990, when he had to build the anti-Iraq coalition in a very short amount of time.

However, intense commitment can also lead to emotional involvement that can create a negative impact on the negotiations. Emotion may cloud the objectivity of the negotiators and lead them to choices that are not well advised. Some commentators have argued that one of the factors that contributed to the hard stance taken by President Bush toward Iraq in the 1990–1991 Gulf War was being dubbed a wimp by *Newsweek* magazine during the 1988 presidential campaign. They contend that Bush's rejection of the negotiation channel in favor of military force against Iraq can be interpreted at least partly as an effort to reduce his wimp image with the American public. Similar arguments have been made about Bill Clinton's actions during the Iraqi weapons inspections crises, especially the Desert Fox operation of the winter of 1998–99: that, facing impeachment and removal from office at home, he eschewed the negotiation channel in favor of air strikes on Iraq.

The injection of ethnicity into the mix of negotiation variables can also have a significant impact on the commitments parties have to particular negotiations and their outcomes. In fact, many of the negotiations that have been described in this book and studied over the years have focused on the resolution of ethnic conflicts and the accompanying claims for resources and legitimacy. The post–cold war period has seen a variety of long-simmering hostilities—such as those among Croats, Muslims, and Serbs and between Serbs and ethnic Albanians in the Balkans—come openly and violently to the fore. Besides its long-standing negotiation efforts in Northern Ireland and the Middle East, the international community is also attempting to continue or expand mediation efforts in Bosnia, Chechnya, East Timor, and Rwanda. In these places and many others, legacies of ethnic hatred and conflict produce perceptual roadblocks to negotiated settlements because of a lack of trust and often a record of bad faith among the parties. In some instances, these legacies are the results of ethnic animosity that dates back hundreds of years. These Balkan conflicts, for example, can be traced back to medieval times.

The potential for misunderstanding is rife when relationships are rooted in emotional perceptions of the "other." Communication in such situations often seems trapped in a negative cycle, with symbolism and innuendo carrying enormous weight. In 1988, when the British tightened controls over the press in Northern Ireland and asked Catholics to "support the law, the British government, and your Queen," the message that Catholics interpreted was closer to "indicate that you are ready to betray friends and neighbors by ceasing to tolerate violent protest by the IRA because loyalty to the crown is important and violence is wrong" (Fisher et al. 1997, 75, 77). Conflicts laced with ethnic threads can raise perceived stakes for the actors involved and increase the likelihood that misperceptions or differing perceptions of the same phenomena will occur and create obstacles to successful negotiations.

As these examples illustrate, when issue involvement becomes emotionally charged at the domestic level, it will complicate the international dimension of the negotiations. Even in policy arenas traditionally considered low politics, controversy can develop as more domestic actors become involved in the process and push hard for negotiated solutions that are favorable to their own particular interests.

The Effect of Crisis

A key factor affecting perceived issue salience in the negotiation arena is the existence of a crisis atmosphere in the decision-making and negotiating environment. Discussed in chapter 2 as a feature of the international system, the impact of crisis on issues is worth mentioning here as well. When core national values are at stake, a situation that often occurs during crises, domestic infighting becomes less important. Crisis situations also tend to focus decision-making attention on a country's chief executive and narrow circle of advisers.

Crisis situations create perceptions of high levels of potential costs to a nation-state. Because crises threaten basic national and societal values, they raise the interest of all policy actors, even if that attention may largely be of only a supportive nature from those outside the executive circle. The UNSCOM case offers an excellent illustration of the ways a crisis atmosphere shapes the course of international negotiations and limits the actors involved in them. As detailed in chapter 1, the primary actors in this set of events were U.S. president Bill Clinton, U.S. secretary of state Madeleine Albright, Iraqi president Saddam Hussein, and his deputy prime minister Tariq Aziz. During the crisis, Albright's high-profile trips throughout the Middle East—aimed at garnering support among the more moderate countries in the region—made the daily news, while pronouncements made by all of these actors received widespread international attention. The negotiations taking place, even if conducted at times by lower-level national policymakers and officials from the UN, and the points agreed to were all clearly authorized and monitored by the highest levels of government. Other domestic-level actors, such as the U.S. Congress, were actively aware of the negotiations but took a backseat. Congress, for example, was—if anything—encouraging stronger action than the Clinton administration was willing to take.

U.S. secretary of state Madeleine Albright is met by Bahraini interior minister Sheikh Mohammed bin Khalifa Al Khalifa as she arrives at the Manama airport November 16, 1997. Albright arrived on a suddenly scheduled visit to thank UN weapons inspectors who had recently left Baghdad. (AP Photo/Hasan Jamal)

This type of high-level political involvement resulted from the perception that the issues at stake in this crisis threatened the core values of the actors. For the United States, those values included international political influence in the region and the Iraqi military threat to allied countries. Iraq was concerned with its sovereignty, Saddam Hussein's stability, its domestic and regional reputation, and the resumption of domestic economic order in the wake of UN sanctions after the 1990–1991 Gulf War. That core values and interests were involved greatly increased issue salience for all parties to the negotiations.

Media Attention

Issue salience can also be affected by the level of domestic and international attention afforded a negotiation issue. As established earlier in this chapter, sometimes this attention is focused as a result of perceived subgroup stakes in an issue area. At other times, such as in crisis situations, there is a tendency for the whole group to rally behind the responses of top leadership. Nonetheless, perceptions of stakes can be greatly swayed by national and international media reporting on an issue. The importance of the media has grown in this era of CNN and the Internet. The "press" now reaches out to people through a variety of different media and fulfills key roles in setting the agendas for top policy officials, providing information on and analyses of international events, and often shaping the opinions held by elites and the public in countries throughout the world.

An example of media impact can be found in the Clinton administration's last-minute decision to send Vice President Gore to Kyoto, as documented in chapter 1. American and international media sources were targeting Bill Clinton and Al Gore as having sold out on the environmental credentials they so carefully crafted during the 1992 election campaign. The Clinton team was clearly in a "put up or shut up" situation in Japan. This made the apparent American negotiation strategy—stall and obstruct—very hard to maintain in the face of media scrutiny. This high level of attention and criticism was a major factor in the decision to dispatch Gore to Kyoto, a trip he had not planned to make.

Media watchers have long debated whether the role of the media is that of political watchdog or lapdog (Rourke, Carter, and Boyer 1996). Sometimes journalists do seem to have been manipulated by political leaders to further the politicians' goals, but at other times journalists blow the whistle on situations about which they feel the public would be interested in hearing. In fact, recent diplomatic history provides evidence of both portrayals. The role of the press following the Tiananmen Square massacre in Beijing, China, in 1989 supports the watchdog characterization. In May and June of that year, pro-democracy student protests took place in Tiananmen Square; the protesters were kept informed through links with other students and peers around the globe. The world community was stunned in June when the Chinese government rolled tanks and troops into the square, killing many protesters and reestablishing firm control over domestic politics. Human rights groups worldwide led the cry for sanctions against the Chinese government and lobbied many governments to link trade with China to political reforms and an improved human rights record.

However, largely out of a fear of losing access to the immense Chinese market, President Bush sent National Security Advisor Brent Scowcroft and Deputy Secretary of State Lawrence Eagleburger on a secret mission just weeks after the massacre to smooth over the harsh rhetoric both countries had been using since the onset of the crisis. When the press got wind of this mission and reported on it, human rights groups and, more generally, the Democratic Party in the U.S. Congress widely took the Bush administration to task. It seemed at the time the president was out of sync with the wishes of the American people regarding these secret diplomatic negotiations and that the press was serving the public interest in making the events public knowledge. Thus, when the media is in watchdog mode, its attention does increase the visibility of the negotiation, thereby increasing its salience. Of course, the case can also be made that the media can be subject to manipulation by decision makers.

At times, the media is used by high-level leaders to achieve their goals in international negotiations, serving as a kind of lapdog. For example, most international trips world leaders take are media events of a high order. These events are staged to influence officials and constituents in their own countries and those of their negotiating partners. When Yasir Arafat and Yitzhak Rabin were photographed shaking hands in the White House Rose Garden in 1994 with President Clinton by their sides, this photo opportunity was staged at least partly to send a signal to all the parties—domestic and international—with a stake in the Arab–Israeli conflict that the two leaders had learned to get along and put many of their differences behind them, and that the United States sanctioned this progress made toward peace.

The Clinton administration provides another example of the connection of media attention to manipulation of international public opinion. In 1997, President Clinton invited the leader of Northern Ireland's Sinn Fein (the political wing of the IRA) to the White House. This was an astounding turnaround for the United States, which up to that point had refused formal contact with officials associated with the IRA, and Britain immediately registered a strong diplomatic protest to this event. But the media swarmed in to capture Sinn Fein's Gerry Adams shaking hands with a smiling Bill Clinton—his green tie visible on St. Patrick's Day in Washington! On the negotiation front, the chance afforded Adams to show that he was a responsible leader paid off for Clinton. Not long afterward, British prime minister Tony Blair decided that perhaps it was time to allow Sinn Fein a chance to sit at the negotiation table in the Northern Ireland talks. Many credit this change in the negotiation setting for the eventual progress made in the peace talks.

CNN: An Uninvited Negotiator?

The press is not usually invited as a player in international negotiations; nonetheless, it often influences negotiation outcomes. The role played by CNN in the events surrounding the Persian Gulf War of 1991 illustrates the way the media can affect the negotiation process—and can even be manipulated by parties to the conflict. CNN's coverage of the Gulf War became quite controversial, even leading one critic to suggest that it change its name to SNN or the Saddam News Network. When the bombing began, one of CNN's correspondents, Peter Arnett, remained in Iraq and reported a number of stories that upset many observers in the United States. Particularly offensive to viewers was Arnett's escorted tour of what the Iraqis claimed was a bombed-out baby formula factory, which the U.S. military insisted was actually a munitions factory and therefore a legitimate military target. Had CNN become an organ for Iraqi propaganda? In its defense, one CNN producer blamed the pressure placed on the contemporary media to report news widely and rapidly, which he claimed creates a tendency to broadcast with inadequate thought to source and implications (Hartford Couraut 1991, A6).

The CNN stories also had some impact on the way the U.S. public and the international audience perceived the war. As for the effect of such media coverage on the negotiations, it can be argued that the graphic presentation of the human tragedies of this war pressured the Bush administration to seek a quick termination to the conflict and to sign a truce agreement that allowed Saddam Hussein to remain in power. In that sense, the media played a significant role in discouraging the Allied Coalition from pushing on to Baghdad and achieving a more definitive victory over Saddam Hussein. In the end, it can be argued that the media presented information in ways that colored perceptions of the conflict around the world and ultimately may even have constrained the decision-making latitude members of the Allied Coalition possessed.

Two-Level Negotiations

As is clear from the discussion in previous sections, the traditional conception of high and low politics issues as they apply to negotiation stakes does not paint a complete enough picture. Thus far, this chapter has argued that issue salience provides an alternate basis and that salience varies depending upon how a series of factors impact the situation—including cost–benefit calculations, the levels of commitment by top leaders and interested domestic parties, the urgency of the situation, and the amount of international media attention focused on the negotiations. The central theme that underlies the presentation of these factors is that the perceptions of various domestic subgroups can heavily impact the overall salience of an issue for political leadership.

On a theoretical level, examination of the interplay between domestic and international politics addresses an age-old question in political science and international relations: what influence do domestic politics have on international relations and vice versa? The remainder of this chapter attempts to address this important question as it relates to international negotiation.

The Impact of Domestic Politics

One way to think about the interplay between domestic and international politics is to place the discussion of issues into the context of what Putnam calls a two-level game. This term suggests that the international negotiation process has two basic components (Putnam 1988, 436):

> **KEY TERM**
>
> **Two-Level Game**   A term used to characterize the double set of negotiations that must be carried out both at the domestic level and at the international level.

Level 1: International—bargaining between negotiators leading to a tentative agreement.

Level 2: Domestic—separate discussions within each group of constituents about whether to ratify the agreement.

Putnam's main objective is to show that there can be a sequence to negotiations, with international negotiations being followed by related domestic negotiations on such matters as ratification. It is important to note, however, that the interaction between the domestic and international negotiation components can also be reciprocal, with the level 2 dialogue often beginning during the level 1 negotiations. At times in the negotiation process, international negotiators will consult with domestic political actors to make sure that what is being discussed at the bargaining table will be acceptable to them during the ratification phase.

Trade negotiations often exhibit the highest degree of domestic involvement in international negotiations because of the impact trade policy has on jobs and the general everyday economic existence of many sectors and individuals within a country. In the United States, the Constitution gives both houses of Congress a role in trade negotiations. Called "non–self-executing congressional–executive agreements," trade agreements require congressional approval by each house after the president signs them. What this means in simple political terms is

> **KEY TERM**
>
> **Fast Track**   Authorization that assures the U.S. president of a congressional vote without amendments on trade negotiations if Congress has been consulted throughout the process.

that there are many more actors and interests involved before, during, and after trade negotiations.

The so-called fast-track authorization process in American trade legislation and associated trade negotiations is designed to ensure that consultation takes place between the executive branch and members of Congress *throughout* the bargaining process and not only at the very end. Assuming consultation takes place, the agreements are to be speedily

NAFTA Negotiations in the United States: A Two-Level Game

No recent example offers more evidence of the impact of domestic politics on the process and outcome of international negotiations than the negotiations and subsequent debate in the United States over the signing and passage of NAFTA in 1992, which allows the free flow of goods and services among Canada, Mexico, and the United States. Creating the world's largest open market, NAFTA appeared to be one more milestone in a long foreign policy career for President George Bush. From a political perspective, however, the pursuit of NAFTA just prior to an election year provided the opposing candidates, Bill Clinton and Ross Perot, with just the issue to hit home on Bush's apparent lack of concern for domestic affairs. Negatively affected industries lobbied hard against the agreement. Even though econometric analysis showed a net increase in jobs for the U.S. economy, many sectors would still be severely impacted by shifts in production facilities and lower-cost competition from south of the border.

In the United States, concerns over NAFTA focused on three main areas—all related in some way to the effects of the agreement on American jobs—demonstrating the strong domestic character of the issue: low Mexican wages, weak Mexican labor standards, and weak Mexican environmental regulations. Labor unions were concerned about the weaker labor laws in Mexico and how that might lead to the export of American jobs by firms looking to establish lower-cost production facilities while still enjoying tariff-free access to the American market. This position was echoed by environmentalists, who feared that firms might relocate production facilities south of the border to take advantage of weaker environmental restrictions.

Thus, when the 1992 presidential campaign rolled around, Bush's opponents were able to latch on to his support of NAFTA as an exploitable political issue. Ross Perot, running as an independent candidate for president, spoke of the "giant sucking sound" that could be heard as American jobs were siphoned to the south. He hit this point hard and rallied significant public opposition to NAFTA through his flamboyant, populist approach to economic matters. While not denouncing NAFTA outright, candidate Bill Clinton pointed to its deficiencies and promised to negotiate a series of side agreements, aimed squarely at assuaging the concerns of crucial domestic political interests that would help win approval for NAFTA in Congress.

After Clinton's election victory, the worker rights and environmental side agreements were negotiated and ultimately signed at a ceremony attended by former presidents Carter, Ford, and Bush. Later that fall, President Clinton held off the opposition—still led by Perot and many Democratic leaders in Congress—to congressional approval of the pact and narrowly won its passage. In many ways, the conglomeration of political actors that supported and opposed NAFTA was a testament to the old adage "Politics makes strange bedfellows."

approved by Congress. If the executive unit fails to engage in this periodic consultation, Congress can revoke the fast-track authorization and make the trade negotiation process more cumbersome for the president's negotiating team by requiring a much more difficult evaluation and approval process throughout the negotiations.

At other times, domestic actors will have sufficient influence to lay out bargaining guidelines prior to negotiations, limiting those directly involved to the pursuit of only certain options during the talks. For example, during the intermediate-range nuclear forces (INF) negotiations under the Reagan administration, other political players in the United States—particularly in the Pentagon—prevented the primary American INF negotiator, Paul Nitze, from cementing the gentlemen's agreement he had made with his Soviet counterpart during their now famous "walk in the woods." Even though the overall force levels they had agreed to would have given the Americans a numerical advantage in total INF warheads over the Soviets in the European theater, Nitze was not able to sell the agreement to hawks in the Reagan administration. The Pentagon insisted that some Pershing II ballistic missiles with quick strike times remain deployed as part of the agreement—no matter what the ultimate warhead advantage for the United States would otherwise be. The "walk in the woods" agreement only allowed the United States to deploy the slower-flying ground-launched cruise missiles (GLCMs) in Europe. Once it was clear that the Reagan administration would not accept the proposal, the Soviets publicly rejected it as well.

Within the two-level-game framework, Putnam explains that the success or failure of negotiations depends upon the existence of overlap between perceptions of acceptable outcomes at both levels of negotiation. He calls this overlap a win-set. The boundaries of a win-set are conditioned by the distribution of power, the preferences, and the possible coalitions among level 2 constituents. Of course, the influence of these level 2 actors on the negotiations will vary depending on the type of political system in which they are operating. Decision makers from authoritarian political systems, for instance, have more power to pursue certain negotiation objectives unilaterally than do decision makers from democratic ones. It is also possible that the negotiators operating at level 1 may manipulate the outcome to try to appease their international negotiation partners, as well as domestic pressure subgroups, even when the interests of each seem diametrically opposed. In the Kyoto

> **KEY TERM**
>
> **Win-Set** The existence of overlap between perceptions of acceptable outcomes at both levels of a two-level negotiation.

negotiations, one explanation for why the United States signed the pact, despite the opposition of many powerful domestic forces, may have been a Clinton administration calculation that the agreement was unrealistic in its targets and that therefore no attempt would ever be made to implement it anyway. The Clinton team knew other countries would also confront this fact, so by signing the pact, the administration was thus able to look like it supported the accord, even though that may not have been the case.

Put simply, for international agreements to be achieved, there must exist some overlap between the set of outcomes acceptable to the international negotiators at level 1 and those preferred by the groups involved at level 2. Without overlap, no final international agreement is possible, either because the domestic constituency will not approve the agreement made at the international level or because what is acceptable as defined by the involved domestic actors proves unacceptable to the other involved country or countries.

The Involvement of Domestic Actors

Earlier in the chapter, it was noted that different international issues are important to different actors or subgroups at the domestic political level. Looking at the relationship of issue salience to the number and types of political actors that get involved in an international negotiation provides another layer of complexity for the salience framework built throughout this chapter.

Referring back to the NAFTA example (see box earlier in chapter), those negotiations present a good example of what can be called a "mixed domestic–international" outcome. Perceived national salience in America was very high, leading a wide array of domestic groups to enter the fray. Negotiators for the United States worked to achieve the win-set discussed earlier, trying to find outcomes that would be acceptable to legislators, labor unions, and environmental interest groups, as well as to Canada and Mexico. This extensive domestic-input factor can be a help or a hindrance to negotiators (Mo 1994, 1995). Obviously, it complicates the process by adding another layer of complexity, but it can also provide leverage with the international parties. If a proposal is not acceptable back home, a negotiator can use the threat of domestic objections to try to squeeze more concessions out of a negotiation partner, particularly when

<table>
<tr><td>

KEY TERM

Chief of Government Model A case where the decision-making power is very much under the control of high-level leaders on both sides of the table.

</td></tr>
</table>

that partner is especially anxious for a quick agreement.

The classic negotiation case in U.S. foreign policy annals is that of the Cuban Missile Crisis. The stakes have arguably never been higher than during this thirteen-day period, when American and Soviet citizens awaited the outcome, perched on the precipice of nuclear war. Yet at the decision-making level, it presents a case of what could be termed a chief of government model—decision making very much under the control of high-level leaders on both sides of the table (Trumbore and Boyer 1998). As is often the case in crisis situations, other domestic actors backed away from or were excluded from the negotiation arena, leaving the positioning to the national leaders in the White House and the Kremlin.

The NAFTA case, then, exemplifies an issue that is highly salient for a broad range of domestic actors, whereas the Cuban Missile Crisis, which was also highly salient for domestic interests, included only a small circle of involved actors—although admittedly very high-level attention. The relationship of salience to domestic involvement can play out in other ways as well. When a broad cross section of citizens does not perceive the negotiations to be very important—as in noncrisis environments with such economic matters as currency valuations—negotiation policies and progress are often in the hands of small groups, far removed from the upper echelons of political leadership. Often, these matters are very routine or highly specialized.

Among the great number of negotiations in the international arena that capture the attention of neither broad cross sections of society nor top leadership are the many routine matters that administrators or bureaucrats handle on a day-to-day basis. Negotiations over foreign aid distributions fit squarely here, except in those rare cases when such decisions become politically charged. Normally, the relative inattention paid means that the narrow group making the decisions ends up with a wide degree of policy-making autonomy and operates largely out of the purview of the public and most other political actors.

In international monetary policy the interplay that exists among central banks, commercial banks, and legislators in many financial capitals of the world provides a good example of an exclusive club working on a highly specialized issue. In Germany, Japan, and the United States, individuals from these various influential posts negotiate among themselves first at the domestic level and then at the international level. Thus, the stakes may be highly salient for that small group of bankers, but monetary policies are widely perceived as issues of low salience for the general public.

Summary

It should be very clear that the answer to the question of who gets involved in negotiations at both the domestic and international levels is determined by how salient the central issue is for political actors. In negotiations among Canada, the United States, and Mexico over the environmental area of NAFTA, the logical actors, based on the domestic salience of the issue, were representatives of the respective governments, of environmental groups—domestic and transnational—of organized labor, and of business groups. The "green" groups worried about lax environmental standards spreading northward, labor groups worried that jobs would move to where the standards are lowest, and business groups wanted to make sure that environmental restrictions would not be made more stringent by virtue of the pact. Returning to the concepts presented at the beginning of this chapter, it is difficult to classify environmental legislation according to the high/low politics scheme, as it is certainly of high political importance to the actors listed above, even if of little interest to many others. More precisely, it is the salience of an issue—its resonance in the domestic arena—that determines the nature and number of actors that become involved.

In addition, the relative power of the domestic actors involved in negotiations on the issue must be taken into account. Some issues that are not broadly salient across an entire political system can gain high-level attention because of the action of a small group of domestic actors. The change in travel plans by Vice President Gore regarding the Kyoto meetings illustrates this point by revealing the relative power held by environmental groups in the United States.

What the examples in this chapter have shown is that there are no simple classification guidelines for understanding how issues affect negotiations. The argument is made for a more complex approach to understanding the ways issues help define negotiations in terms of the involved actors, the intensity of the negotiations themselves, and the possibility for compromise or conflict throughout the negotiation process. The next chapter helps define negotiations even further by examining the strategy and tactics used by negotiating parties to achieve their goals.

Key Web Sites

USAID: http://www.info.usaid.gov/
    (U.S. governmental agency that conducts foreign assistance and
    humanitarian aid)
Public Agenda Online: http://www.publicagenda.org/
    (nonpartisan source of information on public opinion and how to
    read and interpret polls)
U.S. Chamber of Commerce International Policy Statements:
    http://www.uschamber.org/policy/international.html

Statements by Indian prime minister Vajpayee and Pakistani prime minister Sharif about May 1998 nuclear tests:
  India—May11, 1998: http://www.meadev.gov.in/govt/nuclear/official-1.htm
  Pakistan—May 23, 1998: http://www.pakistan-embassy.com/nawazstat.htm
  Pakistan—May 28, 1998: http://www.pakistan-embassy.com/nucstat.htm
  India—May 28, 1998: http://www.meadev.gov.in/govt/nuclear/official-7.htm
    (back-and-forth exchanges between the two countries showing how world leaders attempt to manipulate international political opinion)
The Language of Trade: http://www.usia.gov/topical/econ/language/homepage.htm
    (a glossary of terms used in international trade and trade negotiations, published by the U.S. Information Agency)
Competing Views of NAFTA in the United States—Pro: http://www.usmcoc.org/nafta.html
    (U.S.–Mexico Chamber of Commerce)
Competing Views of NAFTA in the United States—Con: http://www.citizen.org/pctrade/nafta/naftapg.html (Public Citizen) and http://www.aflcio.org/stopfasttrack/index.htm (AFL-CIO)

All of the above sites can be directly accessed from the website for this book: www.icons.umd.edu/negotiating/links.htm

5

The Moves

Negotiation is a game of strategy. As with most games, making the right strategic choices is sometimes the result of luck, but more often the result of the expert movement of the game pieces around the board. Having thus far explored the board, the players, and the stakes in earlier chapters, it is now time to examine the range of possible moves in the game of negotiation—strategies and tactics used in the international arena.

Making moves that will further negotiation goals involves first devising a plan and then choosing tactics to implement it. In the initial stages of the UNSCOM inspections crisis highlighted in chapter 1, for example, the Clinton administration's approach was to try to force the Iraqis to back down and allow inspections. The tactics used included the following: deploying American military forces to the Persian Gulf region; building diplomatic support at the UN and among the moderate Arab states; using the international media to portray Saddam Hussein as an international outlaw; and exerting economic pressure against Iraq by maintaining the UN sanctions originally put in place because of its covert weapons programs and its actions in the Persian Gulf War of 1990–1991.

Although it sometimes appears that a particular negotiation outcome was obvious from the beginning, in fact a range of choices is available to each party at any point in a negotiation. This chapter will explore strategic choices, first by representing them through a number of simple games and then by examining the layers of complexity associated with real-world decision making. The chapter concludes with a comparative analysis of the primary strategic approaches to international negotiation and the tactics associated with each approach.

Modeling Strategic Choices

Negotiation models based in game theory illustrate the array of choices one actor has at any given moment, as well as the way outcomes are dependent upon the choices both or all of the negotiating parties make. Thus, the modeling of strategy and strategic choices is a good way to begin to understand this most critical of negotiation tasks. Because game models presume perfect or full information about the other parties' preferences (see figures below), they are by nature abstractions and simplifications of the real world, but they do help isolate the most important components of negotiation situations. The chapter begins by presenting simple constructions of available choices and then moves on to include additional factors to bring the models closer to real-world complexity.

> **KEY TERMS**
>
> **Simultaneous Game** A game modeled so that the players must make their decisions at the same time.
>
> **Sequential Game** A game modeled so that each player makes a decision at a different point in time.

Since it is important to develop an understanding of negotiation through game theory in a relatively straightforward way, the examples presented below are focused on two main types of negotiation games: simultaneous games, which illustrate the interdependence of each choice on the choices the other players make; and sequential games, which reveal the mounting complexities inherent in action–reaction decision making. The intention here is to get at basic mechanisms of choice as a means of explaining strategy.

Simultaneous Games

In all games, the decisions one player makes are affected by the possible decisions others will make. This issue is a very acute problem for decision makers who find themselves in simultaneous-game situations. It is also a problem, as illustrated below, in sequential games as actors move along the limbs of a decision tree, though not to quite the same extent or in quite the same way as in simultaneous games. This is why decision making in simultaneous games is called interdependent decision making. When decisions are made in an interdependent setting, high levels of uncertainty exist, and that uncertainty becomes the defining characteristic of the decision-making process during the negotiations. The next sections focus on two simultaneous games—the prisoner's dilemma game and the game of chicken—that have been widely applied to international relations situations.

Prisoner's Dilemma

In the classic story of the prisoner's dilemma, the police arrest two suspects for a crime they are alleged to have committed together. The prisoners are held in separate cells and are unable to communicate with each other. They are then individually presented with an offer by the police detectives who are interrogating them about the crime. If one prisoner turns over evidence and testifies against the other prisoner, then the one providing the testimony will go free and enjoy the full proceeds of the crime. Both prisoners realize, however, that if each remains silent, the prosecutors will not be able to make a case against them and both will go free. Being thieves in the first place, both also know that their collaborator is not entirely trustworthy. Thus, there is a risk that the other prisoner will be the one to squeal, sending his or her colleague straight to prison.

Figure 5.1 illustrates the choices and respective numerical payoffs associated with each option available to the prisoners. Each prisoner is presented

Figure 5.1 The Prisoner's Dilemma Game

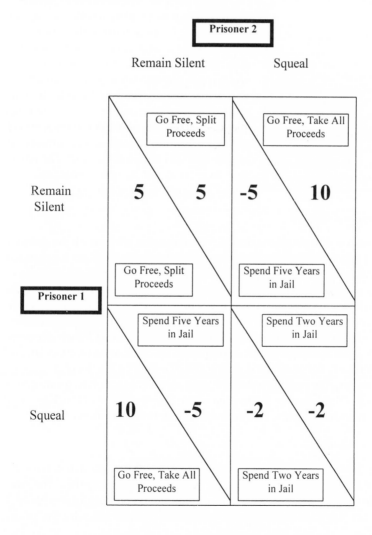

with two choices: remain silent or squeal on the other prisoner. If both prisoners remain silent, they both go free and ultimately split the proceeds from their crime (the payoff of 5 for each). If they both choose to squeal on the other, then both get a prison sentence of two years (represented by the payoff of –2). Each prisoner confronts the possibility that the other prisoner will squeal and produce a five-year prison sentence for the partner (the –5 payoff). Squealing may also yield personal freedom and the ability to lay sole claim to any hidden loot. Faced with this dilemma, the suspects squeal on each other, and both end up in prison for the crime in the classic ending to this story. This is an outcome both suspects could have avoided if they had trusted each other and kept silent. The problem is, however, that each prisoner can see that squealing is the better option, whether the other prisoner squeals or remains silent. In other words, it is the dominant strategy—better for the individual under both possible situations. Herein lies the difficulty: individually dominant strategies lead to worse outcomes—hence the conflict between individual and group rationality.

Many international negotiating situations, from cross-border environmental problems to disputes over markets and free-trade agreements, have been modeled as prisoner's-dilemma situations (Conybeare 1986; Sandler 1997). With environmental issues, for example, the comparison to the prisoner's dilemma rests in the fact that each country involved in the negotiations wishes to promote global environmental quality—in theory. However, no country entirely trusts the other countries involved in the negotiations or wants to bear the cost of implementing and enforcing environmental regulations within its borders. In addition, as discussed in chapter 4, there may also be powerful domestic groups pushing for the adoption of policy that favors their own commercial interests at the expense of environmental quality. Thus, even though all have a basic desire for a healthy environment, many do not wish to bear the cost and in effect choose to squeal on the others by polluting. This collective squealing results in a negative outcome for the world community that might have been avoided if the game and its choices were structured differently and if the actors trusted each other to a higher degree. The possibility for cooperation in such instances will be discussed later in this chapter.

Chicken

The drama of the second simultaneous game, chicken, unfolds as follows: late at night, two drivers sit in cars facing each other from a distance of about half a mile. With the swing of a flashlight, someone on the side of the road signals for both drivers to start driving toward one another as fast as they can. As they get closer, each driver hopes the other will swerve off the road and become the chicken in this test of wills. If neither swerves, the cars crash head-on and both drivers are killed in the high-speed collision. But, in a perverse way, a crash shows both drivers as strong willed and as winners. If one of them swerves, that driver is branded the chicken, humiliated in front of the onlookers, and seen as the loser, even though in a very real sense the chicken is the driver who spared the lives of both players in this game of survival, will, and humiliation.

Figure 5.2 lays out the logic of chicken, illustrating the possible choices and payoffs for each driver. The potential for disaster is manifest when both players drive straight, ending in death for both (–30 payoffs for

Figure 5.2 The Game of Chicken

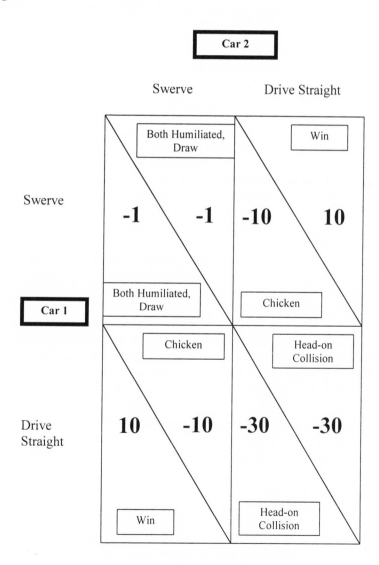

both). Each player is faced with the decision to risk embarrassment and loss of the game, which, if experienced individually, has a negative pay-off (–10). Alternatively, a player can choose to risk his or her life (payoff of –30) for the win (payoff of 10). Unlike the players in the prisoner's-dilemma game, the players in chicken do not have dominant strategies (those better for the individual under both possible situations), so the outcome is not as predictable. In order to win, both players must calculate how strong-willed the other player is and try to push the game one moment beyond where they think the other will take it.

Chicken is often used as a model for negotiations during international crises (Snyder and Deising 1977). Two or more states involved in an international crisis are engaged in a spiraling game of chicken that may escalate to war and ultimately threaten the survival of some or all of the actors. During a crisis, diplomats raise the ante by threatening the use of military force, imposing economic sanctions and bringing many other tools of statecraft to bear to try to force the other nations to swerve off the chosen road of international affairs that formed the basis of the crisis in the first place.

The classic example of this type of brinkmanship is the 1962 Cuban Missile Crisis between the United States and the Soviet Union. When, in the early fall of 1962, American U-2 spy planes photographed evidence of the installation of Soviet intermediate-range ballistic missiles on the island of Cuba, U.S. decision makers—under the leadership of President John F. Kennedy—engaged in a course of action that ultimately forced the Soviets to withdraw the missiles from the island. Tension between the superpowers was extremely high during this crisis, and Robert Kennedy, the president's brother and the U.S. attorney general at the time, later recalled that "the noose was tightening on all of us, on Americans, on mankind, and that the bridges of escape were crumbling" (1969, 97). In the end, after a series of transglobal negotiations between the White House and the Kremlin, the implementation of a U.S. naval blockade around Cuba, and a pledge by President Kennedy to remove American missiles from Turkey, the Soviets swerved and agreed to remove their missiles from the island. The eventual resolution required that an additional issue—the U.S. missiles based in Turkey—be put on the table to defuse the crisis and give the Soviet Union an opportunity to save face and avoid the complete-humiliation payoff of the chicken matrix. This is issue linkage, as described in chapter 2.

In simultaneous games like those described above, each side must make choices at the same time as the other. This simultaneous-decision-making setting means that an understanding of the preferences held by the other side is extremely important, even if information is difficult to obtain in any kind of definitive way. That is why research, intelligence gathering, and analysis have become such important parts of the negotiation process, as all parties to negotiations work diligently to understand the incentives and disincentives (game payoffs) that negotiating counterparts perceive when they enter the negotiation arena. The problem of understanding an actor's negotiation preferences in more detail will be covered in a later section of this chapter. Next, the discussion turns to sequential games and the different negotiation dynamics they present.

Sequential Games

If prisoner's dilemma and chicken represent freeze-frame snapshots of the choices available to negotiators at any particular moment, sequential games illustrate how a series of choices plays out over time. Sequential games model action–reaction processes in order to help reveal the ways international actors react to problems and other stimuli from international affairs. They also demonstrate how those reactions lead to other reactions by even more actors throughout the system.

Traditionally, arms races (Downs, Rocke, and Siverson 1986) and many conflict processes (Wilkenfeld 1991) have been modeled in this way. Arms races, for instance, usually begin when one country feels threatened by the actions or military might of another country. The threatened country decides to buy or build new weapons to increase its own sense of security. But as this country becomes more secure through a weapons buildup, the country that provided the initial threat will likely begin to feel less secure and in turn will want to build up its armed forces. So as both sides respond to the military threats their counterpart poses, neither side becomes more secure over the long term, and both sides engage in a conflict spiral. The 1998 detonations of nuclear weapons first by India and then by Pakistan reflect the rejuvenation of a spiral that had long been dormant. This arms-race cycle has traditionally been termed a security dilemma. Negotiation can play a part in changing the dynamics of an escalating process as both sides seek to reduce tensions—and expenditures on weapons—through negotiating limits to weapons buildups or reductions in weapons stockpiles. SALT and START between the United States and the Soviet Union during the cold war resulted from their joint understanding of the folly of this spiraling arms race.

Sequential choices can be graphically depicted in a decision tree that lays out the options available to negotiators on both sides of the bargaining table at particular points in time. Figure 5.3 depicts a decision tree that models very simply the choices available to U.S. and Iraqi decision makers during the UNSCOM weapons inspections crisis of late 1997–early 1998. Clearly, it is not possible to present all the available options and decision points in the process, but this figure shows how a choice made at the first decision-making point, T_1, constrains the choices available for the other country's decision makers at the second decision-making point, T_2.

This decision tree displays at time T_1 the choice that Saddam Hussein was faced with at the start of the UNSCOM crisis: to prevent inspections or to allow UN inspection teams to examine the various weapons-related sites throughout Iraq. As the tree shows, if Saddam Hussein had chosen to allow

Figure 5.3   Possible UNSCOM Decision Tree

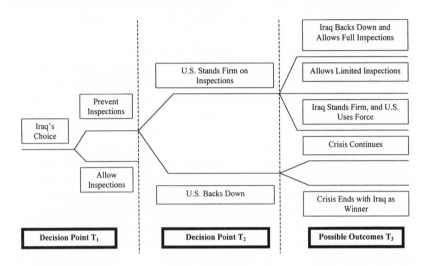

inspections, the crisis would have terminated at the end of T_1. As detailed in chapter 1, however, he chose to prevent the inspections and presented UN and American officials with two basic choices at T_2: to stand firm on the request for inspections of those facilities or back down and allow Iraq to conclude the inspections process. The stand-firm approach was chosen, leaving Saddam Hussein with the three possible outcomes listed on the top tree branches at T_3. Ultimately, though not as immediately as this decision tree indicates, Iraqi officials did allow inspections, but with some important qualifications (see "UNSCOM Plus the Suits" in chapter 1) and not until UN secretary-general Kofi Annan intervened to defuse the conflict.

From the standpoint of negotiation strategy, decision-tree mapping of the options available to the negotiators provides a way to understand the progression of choices that might emerge from an initial decision. This type of strategic decision making can be done by evaluating a decision tree in the reverse direction. This method has been described as the "look ahead and reason back" approach to strategy in sequential games (Dixit and Nalebuff 1991, 34). In the context of the decision tree in figure 5.3, the negotiator must first look at the five possible outcomes labeled at T_3 and rank those outcomes from best to worst. During the UNSCOM crisis, American decision makers—and probably most others on the Security Council—would have ranked the five options in the following order, with number 1 being the most favorable to American and UN interests:

1. Saddam Hussein backs down and allows full inspections;
2. Saddam Hussein stands firm, and the United States uses force under UN auspices;

3. Saddam Hussein allows limited inspections;
4. Crisis continues; and
5. Crisis ends with Iraq as the winner.

For Saddam Hussein and Iraq, the rank ordering would likely have been the exact reverse. As each side examines the potential outcomes and rankings, negotiators try to make choices that push the other side in the direction of their own higher-ranked choices. At T_1, Iraq chooses to prevent inspections since this at least gives it some chance of winning the crisis. At T_2, however, the United States chooses to stand firm on inspections, as this moves toward a set of choices that is less likely to benefit Iraq. Thus, by looking ahead to the set of possible endings to the negotiation episode, negotiators are able to make informed, "backward-looking" choices and adopt bargaining strategies that have the greatest likelihood of providing an optimal outcome for them.

As a result, it is necessary to gain enough information (or intelligence) about the preferences of one's counterpart to be able to predict with a fair degree of accuracy what choice that opponent will make when faced with the options at any point on the tree. Both simultaneous and sequential games allow for the analysis of negotiation strategies. Figuring out how to resolve the game in a way favorable for one's side depends on how well each side is able to manage the degree of uncertainty that exists during the playing of the game. The following section presents an examination of the strategies negotiation actors can adopt to manage uncertainty.

Weighing Strategic Choices

A variety of factors exert an impact on an actor's choice when weighing the relative merits of a particular course of action during a negotiation. As described below in more detail, these factors include: (1) how the actor defines the interests he or she represents; (2) the complexities of the negotiation situation and the ways it influences other relationships; and (3) the degree to which these complexities are linked to one another in ways that either provide opportunities to cooperate or sow the seeds of conflict.

Defining Interests

At the heart of all the games described above is the assumption that individuals act in accordance with their own rational self-interests. An actor is expected to make decisions based on what are perceived to be the best choices vis-à-vis needs for welfare, satisfaction, security, and other key values. To act otherwise would be irrational and run counter to many traditional conceptions of human behavior. To put this point in the context of this book, negotiators and policy makers are assumed to make decisions on the basis of the interests and values held by their con-stituents, whether those interests are based in the nation-state or in the membership of some nonstate entity, such as Greenpeace. Making this assumption about the relationship between rationality and interests pro-vides social scientists with a way of understanding the logic of choice.

It is common in social science to utilize a rough dichotomy when con-ceptualizing interests: a narrow view of national (or actor) interest and a broader or enlightened view of national interest (Lumsdaine 1993). A nar-row definition of interest usually occurs when decision makers and nego-tiators are most concerned with how a particular situation affects political and economic forces at home. For example, at the 1992 Rio Earth Summit, U.S. president Bush declined to sign the biodiversity and global warming pacts developed at that meeting. His decision was based on the impact that these two accords were expected to have on American domestic busi-ness interests; in other words, the Bush administration was concerned pri-marily about the costs American companies would have to bear in the form of pollution control and abatement, as well as other environment-friendly practices, to abide by the agreements. This decision not to sign, while rational from a domestic point of view, was very unpopular in the international community. It was a strong blow against international efforts to act on collective interests regarding global environmental quality.

To return to the prisoner's dilemma game, it is usually argued that con-ceptions of narrow interests explain why the equilibrium—or natural—outcomes in the game are negative or suboptimal ones (prison for both sus-pects in the prisoner's dilemma). In the traditional conceptions of the games, both players are out to safeguard their own narrow interests and thus make their decisions based on individual calculations. But if those interests are somehow transformed from narrow ones to broader ones, then greater opportunity for mutual benefit and positive outcomes becomes possible. This means ending up in the upper-left-hand cell of the game dis-

The Russian Aid Dilemma: A Prisoner's Dilemma?

Since the 1991 fall of the Soviet Union, decision makers in the successor Russian state and other world powers have searched for a way to manage the recurrent Russian economic crises. Beginning with Mikhail Gorbachev's plea for massive financial aid at the Group of 7's (G-7) 1991 London summit and through the August 1998 Russian financial crash, a solution acceptable to all the major actors has been elusive. Russia's economic problems and the related international negotiations exhibit many of the characteristics of the prisoner's dilemma game. The basic issue in the Russian aid dilemma centers on the timing of aid. The Russians view the receipt of economic assistance as an essential element in the country's ability to reform politically and economically; others, including the United States and the IMF, hold that political and economic reform must precede aid to assure that the monies not be wasted in an unstable political and economic system. The basic choices and possible outcomes of this prisoner's-dilemma-type quandary are as follows. (See the payoffs and matrix references in figure 5.1.)

- Sucker payoff for Russia (the –5 payoff value): Russia is required by the donor nations to implement political and economic reforms and then does not get all the aid promised or expected.
- Sucker payoff for the United States and other donors (the –5 payoff value): donor nations give economic aid, and it is not used effectively. Alternatively, aid is given and the Communists or ultranationalists come to power, using the aid to threaten the donor nations.
- Temptation payoff for Russia (the 10 payoff value): Russia asks for and expects aid without political or economic strings attached.
- Temptation payoff for the United States and other donors (the 10 payoff value): donor nations give aid to Russia, but also control its use and help structure the progress of reforms.
- Optimal outcome (upper-left-hand cell): Russia receives aid, reforms take place, and Russian relations with the donor nations are stabilized and improve for the long term.
- Suboptimal equilibrium outcome (lower-right-hand cell): donor nations give little or no aid, little political or economic reform occurs, and hard feelings continue between Russia and the donor nations.

The record of Russian relations with potential aid donors has reflected this set of payoffs and outcomes rather closely, with something approximating the suboptimal equilibrium outcome in evidence. For instance, in September 1998, the U.S. Congress refused to consider President Clinton's request for $18 billion to replenish IMF funds in the aftermath of the Russian and Asian financial crises. Some funds were ultimately made available, but at much lower levels than those perceived as essential for dealing with the Russian crisis (Raum 1998). In December 1998, the IMF followed the lead of its primary donors by withholding additional funds from the Russian government, despite applauding the recovery plans Russian officials detailed (Harrigan, Associated Press, and Reuters 1998). Reflecting Russian frustration, Prime Minister Yevgeny Primakov noted at the time that IMF chief Michel Camdessus "has come with a little briefcase of documents rather than with a huge trunk of cash" (Associated Press and Reuters 1998). And it seems that none of the parties to the aid dilemma has thus far obtained the outcome it desires.

played in figure 5.1 In the prisoner's dilemma, both would escape punishment for the crime. (The box below provides a contemporary example of these kinds of choices, with their associated risks and potential payoffs.)

A number of forces prompt the development of broader conceptions of interest among negotiation actors. Some of these factors depend on the ways actors identify with others involved in the same games. For instance, it is easy to imagine that members of an alliance that has endured over many years will be able to define collective interests far more easily than will newer groups of countries that have not had similar long-term relationships. At the most recent meeting of the Group of 8 (G-8), it was apparent that the expansion of the old G-7 to include post-communist Russia had created some problems in group unity and purpose. The original seven members—Canada, France, Germany, Italy, Japan, the United Kingdom, and the United States—have benefited over time from a significant degree of group cohesion derived from their common identification as the largest industrialized powers in the world and their acceptance of the norms of democratic capitalism. These commonalities result in shared interpretations of international events, which led to shared visions of an international agenda and the policy choices required to fulfill that agenda (Boyer 1999a).

The common bonds were at no time more obvious than after Russia was admitted to the club. The lack of acceptance of the new member was evidenced at the first G-7 (now G-8) meeting that Russia attended in June 1997 in Denver, Colorado. These summits had traditionally been viewed as forums for consultation on macroeconomic policies. The modus operandi had to be changed, however, when Russia's presence demanded that the membership now deal squarely with the problems of transitional market economies. This was an issue at the 1998 summit as well and will likely continue to be a difficult one for the group discussions.

Broad conceptions of interest have also been positively influenced by the creation of international institutions and the development of international norms that govern behavior in some issue areas, as discussed in more detail in chapter 2. The identification of collective interest in relation to nuclear nonproliferation is one such example. The norms and procedures developed since the 1968 signing of the Nuclear Non-Proliferation Treaty show evidence that narrow national conceptions of interest have increasingly become subordinate—for most states—to the desire to safeguard humankind from the proliferation of weapons of mass destruction. The recent international outcry in response to India's testing of four nuclear weapons in May 1998—and Pakistan's subsequent detonation of five—demonstrates the degree to which international sentiment has turned against the national right to possess such weapons. There is, of course, still a great deal of tension between the narrow and broad interests in this case and others like it. Many leaders still argue stridently for national interpretations of defense, prosperity, and other key values, but no one can deny that interdependence has grown in the international system over the last century and, with it, institutions for collective problem solving.

Finally, the determination of narrow or broad interests can also be influenced by the time frame that is considered to be important to decision makers and negotiators. Distinctions between short-term and long-term perspectives are constant factors in international environmental negotiations (for example, Rio in 1992 and Kyoto in 1997). Put simply, short-term interests lead decision makers to pursue agreements that address the immediate economic impact environmental restrictions would have on commercial interests. The comments by American business groups, cited in chapter 4, regarding the impact of the Kyoto protocol on global warming are a case in point. Because many environmental issues do not have direct contemporary effects and because they will become an observable problem only in the future, it is difficult for negotiators to trade their immediate interests for others that are far more abstract. There is a broad, long-term interest in stemming the tide of global warming and the climatic effects it will have, but it is difficult to take this view at the expense of profits and jobs for domestic firms and workers in the shorter term.

Factoring in Complexities

The logic of decision making, as conveyed through game theory, helps illustrate the interdependence of decisions in the negotiation arena. In addition, a number of characteristics or variables at work in a negotiation situation can play out in ways that complicate the negotiations. The following factors—some of which were introduced in the negotiation checklist in chapter 2—complicate negotiations and impact their success. Negotiation or bargaining environments become more complex under these conditions:

- Actors and issues are added to the negotiations, or coalitions form.
- Additional issues are linked to an original issue.
- There is a lack of domestic or constituent consensus about the negotiation goals and/or approach.
- The negotiators themselves do not have decision-making latitude, but must check back with superiors throughout the negotiations.
- The goals and preferences of the negotiation team change during the negotiations due to domestic or international pressure.
- Negotiations involve a mixture of conflictual and cooperative motives or goals.
- Information about other parties' goals and preferences is lacking.
- The situation is perceived as a crisis, thereby increasing the pressure on negotiators.

These factors of complexity illustrate that even when negotiation goals are clearly articulated—and this is not always the case for international actors—a number of forces can thwart their realization. To assume that actor interests are ordered, stable, and prioritized is often unrealistic. The two-level-game notion has helped show that domestic political factors can heavily impact the international negotiation process. The game of chicken shows that actors are also at times confronted with high levels of uncertainty about what choices their negotiation counterparts will make. Interdependent decision making implies that the decisions negotiation actors make are intertwined with each other, but it also means that change by one party makes decisions for others more difficult and outcomes more indeterminate.

Accounting for Long-Term Relationships

Any single negotiation dialogue takes place within the context of the larger relationship between the actors involved. This is part of what we called in chapter 2 the legacy of negotiations. This connection can be useful in a strategic context when negotiators are having trouble seeing ways to resolve conflicting interests at the negotiation table. Negotiators can get a sense of the bigger picture by adding issues (and even actors) from another common negotiation arena to the one in progress (Sebenius 1984) and by considering the longer-term impact of current decisions (Axelrod 1984).

A historical example of the addition of issues can be found in what were called the offset agreements reached by the United States and West Germany during the 1960s over military basing rights. While the United States was providing the dominant share of alliance defense in Europe, West Germany agreed to make offset payments to the United States to help defray the cost of the stationing and maintenance of American forces on German soil. In game theory terms, these are often referred to as side payments. In this way, the American and German negotiators agreed to link the issue of defense of the European central front directly with financial issues. Even though Defense Department officials had been willing to bear the military burden, members of Congress were not as willing, so continuation of the U.S. security role in the region was at least partly sustained by linking defense with finance. Put simply, the Germans made payments so that members of Congress would not put up as much of a fuss over the deployment of American forces in Germany during the cold war.

Awareness of the impact of repeated play has been called in game theory the "shadow of the future" (Axelrod and Keohane 1986, 232–234). Much work has been done on the degree to which negotiators' expectations about future dealings with their counterparts will influence negotiation behavior (Oye 1986). Findings suggest that where the expectation of repeated play is high, the likelihood of cooperative moves becomes greater.

The various rounds of trade negotiations under GATT—established after World War

---

KEY TERM

Reciprocity The practice of countries making in-kind concessions to each other.

II—provide an example of this dynamic. The GATT rounds progressively led to lower tariff barriers to international trade and were based on reciprocity on the part of the countries participating in the negotiations. The success in those negotiations is striking, with tariff barriers to trade reduced from an average of 57 percent in 1947 to an average of about 7 percent in the 1990s (Spero 1990). This long-term commitment to free trade on the part of GATT participants ultimately pushed the negotiators to create the WTO, which superseded GATT on January 1, 1995, as the primary international institution charged with monitoring and promoting free-trade practices around the globe.

Awareness of this larger and long-term relationship, however, can also produce an element of fear. Axelrod (1984, 127) calls this the impact of "tit-for-tat strategies." Again, in the game theory context, the threat that a negotiating partner might reciprocate a squeal payoff sometime in the future provides a negative incentive for such zero-sum strategizing. This can bolster the search for cooperative outcomes on the part of all involved.

Implementing Strategy

The exploration of why decision making and strategy in the negotiation arena are so complex leads to the question of what it means to win in international negotiation. Most situations lend themselves either to zero-sum or to non–zero-sum calculations of interest. Where collective interests are clear—for example, in regard to many environmental problems—the game is usually seen as non–zero-sum. Conversely, where military security is involved, the inclination is toward zero-sum interpretations. This leads negotiators to think, "I won't win here unless you lose." But as discussed above, even some military–security situations are in reality non–zero-sum because of the problems identified in the security dilemma. As one actor builds arms, it produces short-term security for itself, short-term insecurity for its counterpart, and possibly long-term insecurity for all. In other words, since both parties ultimately lose, the arms buildup creates only the illusion of an "I win, you lose" outcome.

It is important to understand what kind of strategic approach makes sense in a negotiation situation. The concept of the zone of agreement helps with this process (Raiffa 1982). As figure 5.4 depicts, each party to a negotiation starts with a minimum position. Visualizing this position in monetary terms helps to show how convergence becomes possible during the course of a dialogue (Raiffa 1982, 48). The car-lot transaction is a commonly used example. The seller opens with a price of $700 ($S_1$), while the buyer opens with an offer of $250 ($B_1$).

KEY TERM

Zone of Agreement The overlapping area of acceptable outcomes for both or all negotiating parties.

Figure 5.4 Zone of Agreement

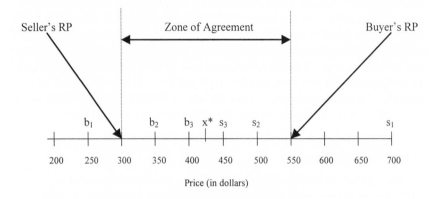

The Negotiation Dance (x* = final contract price).
RP = Reservation Price

Source: Reprinted by permission of the publisher from *The Art and Science of Negotiation* by Howard Raiffa (Cambridge: The Belknap Press of Harvard University Press, 1981).

They then trade concessions and make second offers of $500 and $350. Their final offers to one another are $450 ($S_3$) and $400 ($B_3$). Not surprisingly, when they are this close to making a deal, they decide to split the difference and close the deal at $425. It is important to note, however, that there is a zone of agreement only if the lowest price the seller will accept (his reservation price) is less than the highest price the buyer will pay (her reservation price).

But if this notion is converted to the world of international negotiation—where the currency is national interests however they are defined—finding any clear zone of agreement can be difficult. This is particularly true when actor preferences along a negotiation continuum, such as that displayed in figure 5.4, are intensely held. That is, while it might seem obvious that the rational solution is to split the difference between initial bargaining positions—such as those depicted by S_1 and B_1—one or both actors may be strongly wedded to the initial positions and not wish to move much from them. In such cases, where it is difficult for negotiators to identify common interests or a possibility of movement, there may be no zone of agreement. Negotiators will then tend to adopt a more competitive negotiation strategy, pursued through various "hard" negotiating tactics.

If there are common interests or a possibility of movement away from initial positions, or if there is a will to try to find—or create—a zone of agreement through the use of linkage or a broadening of conceptions of interests, negotiators will engage in collaborative negotiation, using interest-based bargaining techniques. The following sections are structured around the basic dichotomy between competitive and collaborative approaches to negotiation, including various examples of each.

It should be noted that underlying the discussion is an examination of the use of power by negotiators. As discussed in chapter 2, the successful use of power to achieve goals depends on the situation, the relative balance of capabilities between the involved actors, and changes in the structure of the international system itself. Power, after all, is situational, multidimensional, relative, and dynamic, and, as a result, negotiators must gauge how and when to use their power in overt and covert ways. Power tactics are generally overtly used in competitive situations and covertly used in collaborative ones. In collaborative situations, however, power is used more to persuade than to coerce a negotiation counterpart into an agreement.

Competitive Negotiation

Although it would be a cheerier world if only positive incentives were needed to induce cooperation and agreement, it is clear that negotiations often take a negative turn and a variety of sticks—lethal and otherwise—are used to achieve desired goals. As realists have often reminded us in the political science literature, it is naive to assume that everyone will play by the rules of the game. Similarly, it can be foolish to believe that all actors are persuaded by the notion of collective interests. It is often determined, therefore, that the rational approach to an international negotiation situation is a competitive one. Positional bargaining and adversarial and coercive diplomacy are all examples of the implementation of a competitive strategy in negotiation situations.

Positional Bargaining

As mentioned above, sometimes a negotiator represents an international actor that has identified only one desirable outcome to a situation and, as a result, puts that outcome forward and refuses to move away from it. For example, in the zone of agreement case, what if the seller did not back away from his opening position and said instead, "I'll only accept $700 for the car"? In international negotiations, it may be the case that the negotiator's domestic constituents will accept only that outcome or it may be that legal or other constraints rule out other agreements. During the 1962 Cuban Missile Crisis, President Kennedy reasoned that a zero-tolerance stand—no Soviet missiles in Cuba—was the only stand that would allow him to keep the White House in the 1964 election. Given the vehemence of American anticommunism during the 1950s and 1960s, any concession that the U.S. public and Kennedy's political opponents might perceive as soft on communism would have been political suicide. As a result, hard positional bargaining was the only real option

---

KEY TERM

Positional Bargaining
Negotiating stance where actor identifies only one desirable outcome and refuses to move away from it or consider any other options.

available to the president regarding the missile deployment. Although Kennedy did find ways to introduce flexibility into the negotiations, he never backed down from his bottom-line demand: the missiles had to go.

Adversarial Diplomacy

Adversarial diplomacy occurs when the interests of two or more countries clash, but when there is little or no chance of armed conflict. Negotiations over economic issues—market shares, methods for dealing with trade imbalances—and, more recently, negotiations over intellectual property rights (CDs and software, for example) have produced the most prominent examples of adversarial diplomacy in recent years.

During much of the 1990s, for example, the United States and Japan have been at odds over America's efforts to penetrate Japan's domestic market. The dispute became particularly tense in June 1996 during a series of negotiations over U.S. access to the Japanese automobile market. Ultimately, the Clinton administration threatened the imposition of a 100 percent import surcharge on Japanese luxury cars. On the brink of this potentially devastating blow to some key manufacturers (which actually had operations in both countries), the two sides relented and returned to the negotiation table. Cowed by the degree to which their automobile sectors had become interdependent and aware that their larger cooperative relationship in the world was at stake, both parties quickly accepted a face-saving agreement.

The practice of adversarial diplomacy often involves significant threats of sanctions, such as those the United States utilized in the automobile case. Other tactics or tools associated with this form of diplomacy range from imposing strict deadlines on negotiations to threatening the cessation of diplomatic contact. There is a continuum of such tactics, ranging from symbolic measures aimed at the arena of public opinion, to those more activist in nature, where threats are actually translated into concrete actions. These tactics can include the actual imposing of economic and political sanctions or the pulling of an ambassador from a foreign capital.

Coercive Diplomacy

Despite the end of the cold war, the use of military force in the international system is still common. Instability in Asia in the wake of the Indian and Pakistani nuclear detonations of 1998, ethnopolitical strife in Africa, and conflict in Europe over post-communist state-building efforts all point to the continued existence of a nonpacific world in the current unipolar international system. It is clear that many international actors continue to view military force as a primary way of achieving their goals in contemporary international affairs. Thus, the threat of military force—and its ultimate use, if deemed necessary—remains a requisite tool of international affairs (see, for instance, discussions by Haass 1997; George 1997; and E. Cohen 1997). The discussion below focuses on understanding how force can be used as a tool at the negotiation table.

A good example of coercive diplomacy is the UNSCOM case referred to throughout this book. During the entire course of the crisis, the atmosphere was extremely hostile and the threat of military force was overt on the parts of both the Americans and the Iraqis. The photographs in the world media of U.S. naval vessels steaming into the Persian Gulf and warplanes on alert status at bases throughout the Middle East were

---

KEY TERM

Coercive Diplomacy
Negotiating stance involving the threat of force or limited use of force as a tool at the negotiation table.

---

ubiquitous. Both parties attempted to use the threat of military force to intimidate the other party into changing its stance. Indeed, it was with the direst warnings of an imminent American attack that Kofi Annan finally traveled to Baghdad to try to restore the diplomatic channel.

But the use of military force or its threatened use can also have a more subtle impact on negotiations. At the 1945 Potsdam Conference attended by U.S. president Harry S. Truman, Soviet premier Josef Stalin, and British prime minister Winston Churchill, Truman mentioned to Stalin that the United States had just developed a new weapon of mass destruction: the first atomic bomb. Though the bomb was used only against Japanese forces in the Pacific, the mention of its development to Stalin was also a signal of U.S. power and political desires for the postwar period. In this way, the bomb was meant to keep the Soviets in their place, particularly as the victorious powers wrangled over the postwar European political landscape. It also gave birth to the U.S.–Soviet nuclear arms race that would define East–West relations for the next forty-five years.

Collaborative Negotiation

When negotiators are able to identify common interests and use them as the basis for a dialogue, the approach is what is described as collaborative or problem-solving. The strategy is to emphasize common ground while downplaying areas of contention. To a great extent, this approach necessitates a willful change of the character of the negotiation game. The anarchic nature of the international system has traditionally lent itself to relative gains or "beggar thy neighbor" outlooks. This is why a competitive stance in the negotiation arena is more natural to nation-states in particular. Nonetheless, collaboration does frequently emerge, especially among actors exhibiting high levels of interdependence and some sense of long-term, collective interest.

Changing the game so that the focus is on broad rather than narrow conceptions of interest and directing it toward mutually acceptable negotiation outcomes rather than clear-cut victories involves the enhancement of communication between the parties and the construction of trusting relationships. As Winston Churchill, British prime minister during World War II, once remarked, "To jaw-jaw is always better than to war-war" (as quoted in Freeman 1997b). Churchill was alluding to the need to keep the lines of communication open between opposing parties—a crucial part of the negotiation process.

Effective communication is particularly important during crisis negotiations. This was evidenced after the Cuban Missile Crisis by the superpowers' creation of a hot line. Frightened by the communication mishaps that characterized the crisis at critical junctures, the White House and the Kremlin signed the hot line agreement of 1963 to ensure a permanent link between them. Often depicted in films as a red phone (although originally merely a Teletype machine), it boosted confidence in Washington and Moscow about the reduced possibility of deadly misunderstandings by allowing direct, intercontinental communication between the leaders of each superpower.

Interest-based bargaining, informal or track-two diplomatic approaches, and the injection of new insights through mediation provide three alternatives to the tools of the competitive negotiator.

Interest-Based Bargaining

When one conjures up images of negotiators, it is easy to think of them as being soft or hard in their approaches. For example, U.S. president Franklin Roosevelt has often been characterized as being too soft a negotiator at the Yalta Conference in 1945. His conciliatory approach to negotiating with Soviet premier Josef Stalin is commonly construed as one of the reasons why the Soviets were able to consolidate power in Eastern Europe after World War II and establish a political–military hold on the region until 1989. By contrast, George Bush's hard stance in refusing to back down and allow Saddam Hussein a face-saving retreat after his ill-conceived 1990 invasion of Kuwait effectively closed off the negotiation channel in that case. Although the United States was triumphant on the battlefield, critics of the Bush strategy lamented the loss of civilian life on the Iraqi side and argued that negotiations should have been given more of a chance.

In the well-known book *Getting to Yes* (1991), Roger Fisher and William Ury of the Harvard Negotiation Project argue that neither soft nor hard negotiating positions are likely to produce good outcomes. They call their take on interest-based bargaining "principled negotiation" and argue that the

---

KEY TERM

Interest-Based Bargaining
Negotiating stance that focuses on trying to understand the needs of the other party and finding areas of common interest.

focus must be taken off of positional negotiating and put instead on efforts to find areas of common interest among the actors.

To move beyond the problems of positional bargaining, Fisher and Ury suggest four specific moves:

- Separate the people from the problem;
- Focus on interests, not positions;
- Invent options for mutual gain; and
- Insist upon using objective criteria to judge the merits of possible solutions.

These are all measures that can be used to try to build trust among negotiation adversaries and boost their confidence in the negotiation process.

The idea of separating the people from the problem suggests that negative emotions and perceptions of the "other" (see chapter 3) be removed from the negotiation table to the greatest extent possible. Instead of looking at one's counterparts as enemies, it is better to perceive them as mere representatives of interests—maybe even interests that do not oppose your own. By getting to know one's counterparts on a personal level, an understanding of those interests and the needs underlying them becomes possible. Indeed, the centerpiece of principled negotiation is a focus on interests and needs rather than on positions. An excellent real-world example of this approach is the Israeli–Egyptian negotiations over the Sinai Peninsula. The positions of the two states were diametrically opposed—Israel insisting on keeping the territory it had won in the 1967 Six-Day War and Egypt demanding the territory's return. Progress was achieved during the Camp David negotiations in 1978 only when the American mediator, President Jimmy Carter, got the negotiating teams to focus on underlying interests. Ultimately, it was determined that Israel's need was for security in the form of a buffer zone, while Egypt's need was to reassert its sovereignty, for the benefit of domestic and regional concerns, by regaining lost territory. Framing the problem in this way allowed an eventual solution to present itself. Ultimately, it was clear that the needs of both sides could be met by making the Sinai a totally demilitarized zone, under the control of Egypt but closely monitored by the UN.

The idea of the demilitarized zone is an excellent example of what Fisher and Ury call an "option invented for mutual gain" (1991, 56). Brainstorming about the needs and interests of both sides and the nature of the problem itself allowed the negotiators to find ways to harmonize their interests, despite their seemingly total divergence. This solution allowed both sides to achieve their goals, while still saving face in regard to the compromise they had made.

Finally, demilitarization in this case represented an objective standard or criterion—from the security lexicon—upon which agreement could be based.

Although such standards cannot be found for all areas of international negotiation, there are many cases where they can be found and used. In the human rights arena, the twin covenants on civil/political and economic/social rights fulfill this need. In the environmental arena, scientific judgments and definitions, as well as international laws and legal traditions, provide guidelines for states seeking to find fair solutions to international disputes.

Track-Two Diplomacy

One of the most innovative methods for building trust among negotiators is the growing use of track-two or unofficial diplomacy in a variety of international conflict settings. This type of negotiation usually involves nontraditional diplomats and nontraditional settings. The strength of the track-two approach on conflict resolution is based on the idea that informal negotiations allow the parties "to come together more easily to explore mutual fears, grievances and demands" (Rasmussen 1997, 44). Track-two diplomacy also provides the opportunity for tentative negotiation offers to be floated, policy linkages to be explored, and other barriers to successful negotiations to be broached in ways that formal negotiations might preclude. A variety of actors can participate in these informal negotiations as well. Examples range from third parties, such as scientists exploring hypothetical issues and engaging in dialogues about them, to networks of low-level officials from conflicting parties whose participation in negotiations is much less controversial than that of their national political leaders. The so-called Oslo negotiations between the Israelis and the Palestinians have quickly become a classic example of track-two diplomacy and are discussed in detail in the accompanying box.

Other examples of confidence-building measures and informal diplomacy have also had notable effects on the reduction of tensions among negotiating parties and have helped to move talks from stalemate to agreement. Confidence-building measures were employed for years during the cold war as ways of reducing superpower tensions in Europe. Both sides made a habit of informing the other of military exercises and would often use only blanks in weapons during such exercises. Moreover, military officers were routinely exchanged as ways of personalizing the forces of the other side in an effort to pull the countries away from the faceless stereotypes and xenophobia that at times cause international tensions to flare.

KEY TERM

Mediation An outside perspective brought in to help find ways to resolve a deadlocked conflict when parties desire progress but cannot resolve issues themselves.

Mediation

A last option under the heading of collaborative approaches is the use of mediation to help negotiators find a zone of agreement. This form of third-party intervention (as discussed in chapter 2) often succeeds when a negotiation has reached a

Track-Two Diplomacy: The Oslo Agreement

One of the most notable recent successes of the track-two approach was the breakthrough in Israeli–Palestinian negotiations from 1992 to 1993. As has so often been the case in the protracted Israeli–Palestinian conflict, the momentum in the peace process by the end of the 1990–1991 Persian Gulf War had given way to stalemate by late 1992. Through the intervention of Norwegian diplomats, however, the talks were jump-started in September of that year. The mediation of Norway's foreign minister, Johan Joergun Holst, facilitated this approach. The track-two talks, held near Oslo, created opportunities for close relationships to develop between Israeli and Palestinian representatives in these secret, unofficial negotiations. The atmosphere was deliberately kept intimate in an effort to increase the chances for a breakthrough. Israelis and Palestinians "shared plates of Norwegian salmon and wandered together in nearby woods" (Fedarko 1993, 51). The model developed by the Norwegians represented a stark contrast to the traditional one then being applied in the U.S.-sponsored Madrid negotiations.

It was within this informal environment that the details of a peace agreement between the two parties were examined and finalized. After the process became public, videotape even showed negotiators from both sides lightheartedly playing with Holst's toddler son during some of the sessions. From this relaxed environment, agreements emerged that accomplished the following:

- Israel recognized the PLO as "the representative of the Palestinian people."
- The PLO denounced violence and recognized Israel's right to exist.
- Both sides agreed to a five-year plan, to culminate in 1998 with the creation of Palestinian self-rule in the West Bank and Gaza.

Although the assassination of Israeli prime minister Yitzhak Rabin in October 1995 and the subsequent election of a new, more conservative prime minister sidetracked progress toward completely fulfilling these agreements, the achievements of this track-two approach are nonetheless striking in the context of the long-term hatred and distrust that have characterized the conflict for nearly fifty years.

point of deadlock. An outside perspective or "new blood" may be needed to help find ways to resolve the conflict of the moment (Princen 1992). In this vein, mediation is undertaken at a point during the negotiation when the parties desire some form of progress but find it beyond their capabilities to create that progress or to make it occur within the necessary time frame. The role of Kofi Annan during the UNSCOM crisis is one example of how the intervention of a third party can create opportunities for compromise and de-escalation that did not exist when only the main parties to the negotiation are involved.

To achieve success in deadlocked negotiations, mediators have a number of tactics at their disposal. These mediation tactics can be divided into three broad categories: communication, formulation, and manipulation (Bercovitch 1997, 137–38). Communication strategies, Bercovitch argues, deal with the perceptions of all parties to the negotiation that they are able to speak freely and be heard by the other parties. Thus, a mediator will need to build trust among the actors to reestablish a working relationship among parties that may have become hostile and unwilling to talk. Moreover, a mediator must also create a forum for the discussion of new and innovative ideas regarding the problems at hand. The role of President Carter in the Camp David negotiations discussed above is a good example of how a mediator can help facilitate communication and the exploration of new options for conflict resolution.

A mediator can also shape the process and substance or the formulation of the negotiation. This is done by encouraging the parties to deal with simple issues first and only then work toward the more difficult and complicated ones. It also means identifying potential common interests and compromises that may serve the purposes of all involved, including assuring the secrecy of negotiations to protect the parties' reputations. The Oslo mediation by Norway's foreign minister, Holst, exhibited many of these approaches. Before addressing the major issues, the negotiations first had to proceed to a point where the Israeli Knesset would make it legal to negotiate with the Palestinians. The secret talks also served the purpose of highlighting the high costs that both sides would continue to incur if the Intifada protests and the Israeli responses to the uprising continued into the foreseeable future. More recently, U.S. president Clinton attempted to mediate the stalled Israeli–Palestinian negotiations (implementation of the Oslo agreement discussed above) by combining mediation techniques with a track-two atmosphere.

Finally, a mediator's ability to use his or her position to obtain an agreeable outcome to the problem represents the third tactic: manipulation. The mediator can take personal responsibility for the concessions made so that the parties' constituents can "blame" someone else aside from their own negotiators; can use threats, promises, and other incentives to promote cooperation and agreement; and press parties to show flexibility on certain issues. In many ways, this set of tactics depends quite heavily on the reputation of the mediator in the international arena and, more specifically, within the current set of negotiations.

What all this means is that, at times, successful mediation is dependent upon the role of the mediator within world affairs. Sometimes, intervention

Sunday, October 18, 1998. President Clinton (R), with Israeli prime minister Benjamin Netanyahu at the Wye River Plantation Talks. Credit: White House photo.

by a representative of a great power is required to push a resolution to the final stages. The role of the United States as the dominant political–military power in the world today most certainly had an impact on the success of the Dayton Peace Accords efforts. American initiatives prompted these negotiations after other international interventions had proven unsuccessful. Without the muscle of the United States, it is unlikely that an agreement could have been achieved at that point in time. As this implies, even in collaborative negotiation settings, power relationships have an impact on helping some negotiation actors move toward compromise and the exploration of new options to conflict resolution.

Summary

Negotiators must account for a variety of factors when they choose their strategies and tactics for use in a particular situation. Negotiations among friends differ greatly from those among adversaries; negotiations (and

The Wye River Negotiations: Mediation in a Track-Two Setting

Many observers of the Middle East peace process have viewed the election of Benjamin Netanyahu in May 1996 as an event that took the process backward a few steps. Certainly, the march toward peace between the Israelis and the Palestinians was exceedingly slow from Netanyahu's election until January 1998, when President Clinton stepped in to try to jump-start the stalled negotiations. After more than six months of relatively futile exchanges about sticking points in the implementation of the Oslo Accords (see previous box), Clinton hosted Netanyahu and Palestinian Authority president Yasir Arafat at Maryland's Wye River Conference Center in October 1998 for nine days of negotiations.

For Clinton, under siege at home in the impeachment hearings, the intensely difficult negotiations provided an opportunity to show the nation and the world that he could conduct business as usual and that American prestige in this most difficult of international regions was alive and well under his watch. His determination to fulfill his mediation role was clear when he arrived at the center on the last scheduled day of talks and declared to all present, "We are going to stay here until we finish this. We are going to finish it today or we're not going to finish it" (Schmemann and Erlanger 1998, 14). He then devoted all of his personal attention and energy to the issues yet to be resolved.

Of particular interest in the approach that Clinton and his team took at the Wye River talks are the obvious lessons they drew from the successful Norwegian facilitation efforts at the track-two Oslo talks. Observers at Wye River looked on as Arafat took a long bicycle ride and as negotiators were presented with T-shirts that compared the negotiations to the movie *Groundhog Day*, where every day repeats itself. Secretary of State Madeleine Albright sought cover under this (forced) informal setting when she telephoned Netanyahu at 2:25 one morning, ostensibly to wish him a happy birthday (Schmemann and Erlanger, cited above). What will be remembered long after all the arguments and moments of levity, however, is the enormous effort Jordan's ailing King Hussein made to come to Wye River, at Clinton's invitation, to help break the deadlock. The speech he gave, his last official appearance on behalf of Middle East peace, was one of the key elements in moving negotiators toward the mutual acceptance of the Wye River Memorandum, signed at the White House on October 23, 1998.

their resulting choices) exhibiting limited opportunities for communication among parties differ from negotiations where the parties regularly and easily communicate with one another; and negotiations involving a mediator differ from those where only the main parties are involved. In each setting, negotiators, decision makers, and the constituents who give them their authority must make different calculations.

In many ways, this chapter has attempted to provide an appreciation of the complexity inherent in determining and understanding the choices made within negotiations. In particular, the interdependence of decision making that develops during negotiations means that a decision a particular negotiation actor makes is seldom singular or discrete; instead, it is only part of the process that produces an outcome, woven into a fabric comprising the decisions other parties make at a variety of points along the way. As a result, negotiators must choose their strategies and tactics carefully and weigh their choices in an environment fraught with uncertainty and ambiguity. Then again, it is this ambiguity, when combined with the skill of the negotiator, that makes international negotiation and diplomacy the interesting and often unpredictable "game of kings."

Key Web Sites

Strategy and Conflict: An Introductory Sketch of Game Theory: http://williamking.www.drexel.edu/top/eco/game/game.html (an accessible overview of the main concepts in the field, by Roger A. McCain of Drexel University)

The Prisoner's Dilemma: http://ucsub.Colorado.EDU/~danielsm/PD/PD.html

Chronology of the Cuban Missile Crisis: http://www.seas.gwu.edu/nsarchive/nsa/cuba_mis_cri/cmcchron.html (a listing of major events before, during, and after the crisis from the National Security Archives)

Interview with Robert McNamara: http://www.seas.gwu.edu/nsarchive/coldwar/interviews/episode-10/mcnamara1.html (McNamara discusses the Bay of Pigs and the Cuban Missile Crisis for CNN's *Cold War* series.)

Overview of the India–Pakistan Conflict: http://www.washingtonpost.com/wpsrv/inatl/longterm/southasia/southasia.htm (*Washington Post* Special Report)

Group of 7–8: http://www.g7.utoronto.ca/

Wye River Peace Talks: http://www.usis-israel.org.il/publish/peace/october98/ (statements and documents from the Wye River negotiations from the U.S. Information Service, Israel)

Carter Center Conflict Resolution Program: http://www.CarterCenter.org/
    cr.html
    (highlights mediation and peacemaking efforts of the Carter
    Center)
Earth: 2025: http://games.eesite.com/
    (a free, interactive strategy game that allows players to try run-
    ning a country)

All of the above sites can be directly accessed from the website for this book:
http://www.icons.umd.edu/negotiating/links.htm

6

Outcomes

One of the aims of this book is to show that in some respects the diplomatic arena is a far different place today than it was even ten years ago. Some of the catalysts for change occur at the international system level, including the end of the forty-five–year cold war, the ethnic fragmentation of some previously strong states, and a proliferation of issues now part of the negotiation dialogue among states. International negotiations are further complicated by the existence of considerable domestic pressures on the foreign policies of states. Decisions made at the nation-state level about greenhouse gas emissions and control of HIV–AIDS, for example, are international in consequence, making them part of the new dual-track policymaking of states.

Identifying Important Trends

The negotiation landscape is greatly affected by the same large forces that are reshaping all social and political relationships in the contemporary era: the information and communication revolution and its accompanying mass mobilization of citizens. Access to news and knowledge has increased at astonishing rates in every region of the world—including sub-Saharan Africa, which is just beginning to benefit from public and private international endeavors designed to catch it up. International media sources provide nearly instantaneous reporting on events around the world, greatly increasing the number of people watching negotiations and, in some cases, the number of people participating. Mass electronic mail messages sent to delegations at the Kyoto climate talks from concerned members of non-governmental "green" groups around the world attest to the power of the new Internet-based communication channel, to name one notable example.

The calculus of national interest, the foundation of all foreign policy decisions, today resembles more of a labyrinth than the simple high–low categorization of a bygone era. The latitude of policymakers at the nation-state level is constrained by the intense, two-level negotiation games in which they often find themselves embroiled. Strong domestic input from concerned citizens and, in some cases, substate actors and so-called substitute states has infringed on the diplomatic purview of states. The importance of an issue to national interest is no longer a simple starting point for negotiation decisions, as there is no longer anything simple about the notion of national interest.

As new actors, issues, and forms of interaction are introduced into the diplomatic arena, policymakers must be retrained in the art of negotiation. The results of various strategies have been studied, plotted, and, through the game theoretic approach, even modeled. These results show that cooperative approaches can sometimes be used in place of competitive ones to head off destructive standoffs and dangerous escalations (chicken scenarios) and to build opportunities for trust to enhance communication and collective problem solving among parties (prisoner's dilemmas). Longitudinal analyses of conflicts and the negotiations that have attempted to resolve them demonstrate that outcomes satisfactory to both sides, rather than those that represent a win for one and a loss for another, tend to be more long-lasting.

This search for non–zero-sum or win-win outcomes is aided by some new approaches in the diplomatic repertoire, most notably the track-two, informal negotiation setting. In its pure form, this is the Oslo-type forum, where nongovernmental parties from the opposing sides work to resolve problems. The influence of the trademark informal setting is felt in a new adaptation of track two as well: a hybrid model, characterized by more traditional negotiators, but at work in an informal setting. This was the approach at the United States–mediated Dayton Peace Accords to resolve the Bosnia conflict and at the Wye River talks between the Israelis and the Palestinians, also mediated by the United States.

Yet for all of these vaunted changes in the diplomatic realm, there are counterexamples of authoritarian leaders ordering ruthless attacks on internal and external enemies who stand in the way of personal aspirations. Such individuals remind us that—to a great extent—the more things change, the more they stay the same. Indeed, traditional diplomacy (high politics, top leaders, competitive negotiation strategies) is a mainstay of the diplomatic toolbox. With this in mind, it is clear that the analytical tools and frameworks applied to the understanding of international negotiation must be broad enough to encompass both new and traditional diplomacy and flexible enough to account for the presence or absence of certain characteristics—media attention, high domestic salience—across cases.

Analyzing Real-World Cases

The study of diplomacy inevitably leads to a clearer understanding of the key relationships among state and sometimes nonstate actors. Regrettably, the opportunity to apply what has been learned is continual, with new conflicts and negotiation cases—or recurring ones—appearing in the news each day. This book has examined a number of particularly high-profile examples—the ongoing international climate negotiations, the U.S.–Iraqi standoff, the Israeli–Palestinian peace talks, NAFTA, and the Northern Ireland talks, among others—to illustrate key negotiation concepts and the important diplomatic trends discussed above. In addition, it offers an organizational metaphor for the sorting of cases: that of a board game, with a board (setup), players (important actors), stakes (issues and their salience for players), and moves (strategies and tactics). Among the key elements of the negotiation process that the analogy helps to elucidate are the importance of individual personalities to the proceedings, the extent of domestic-level input into the negotiation positions of the various parties, and the degree to which the negotiation represents a unique encounter among the parties, as opposed to just one more episode in an unfolding saga.

One way to apply what has been learned in this book is to take a case from today's (or any day's) headlines and plug it into the analytical framework that is presented. The failed Kosovo peace negotiations in Rambouillet, France, in February 1999 offer a striking example.

The Game

Background

In October of 1998, the American envoy to Bosnia, Richard Holbrooke, went to Belgrade seeking a cease-fire in the Yugoslav province of Kosovo. The struggle between the ethnic Albanian population and the Serb-dominated Yugoslav government, led by Slobodan Milosevic, had already produced thousands of casualties and hundreds of thousands of displaced persons. The cease-fire Holbrooke achieved did not hold, however, leading the United States and its NATO allies to declare that if a negotiated settlement to the conflict were not reached, there would be a bombing campaign against Serbia.

Setup

This pressure for negotiations led to the three-week-long Rambouillet negotiations in February 1999 between Serb and ethnic Albanian representatives.

The talks were organized by the six-nation Balkans Contact Group (United States, Russia, Germany, Britain, France, Italy), whose diplomats acted as mediators.

Players

The main parties to the negotiations were the Yugoslav government representatives and the ethnic Albanians, represented by political leaders and the Kosovo Liberation Army (KLA), a rebel group organized to fight the Serb forces. U.S. secretary of state Madeleine Albright engineered the mediation effort, assisted by diplomats from the Contact Group and, after a deadlock in talks, by such special envoys as former U.S. senator Bob Dole.

Stakes

For Milosevic and the Serbs, sovereignty over the remaining territory of Yugoslavia—their territorial integrity—has always been at stake in this conflict. For the ethnic Albanians, their physical safety and survival in the short term and their ability to gain autonomy and eventual independence from Serbia in the long term are at the heart of the conflict.

Moves

The western proposal on the table in Rambouillet would have granted substantial autonomy to the people of Kosovo but would have stopped well short of independence. It would have guaranteed peace in the province by sending in a NATO peacekeeping force. In essence, the plan suggested that the ethnic Albanians compromise on their demand for immediate and full independence and that the Serbs compromise on their pledge never to allow NATO troops onto their territory. When both sides balked at the idea of concessions, the Contact Group sponsors applied more pressure. They made it clear that if the Kosovars signed on and the Serbs did not, NATO would initiate a bombing campaign against Serbia as punishment. This pressure failed to achieve its desired goal. The Kosovar Albanian side did eventually sign the agreement, but Milosevic fatefully refused, plunging Europe into war.

Negotiation Checklist

The Rambouillet example can be further analyzed using the factors from the negotiation checklist in chapter 2. Matching the Rambouillet case to the concepts produces some compelling findings, including the unique nature of third-party intervention in this example: the six-nation Balkans Contact Group worked on the diplomatic front, while NATO worked as the enforcer, issuing threats before and during the negotiations—threats that were acted upon following the breakdown of the talks. The heterogeneous composition of the ethnic Albanian negotiation team is also noteworthy, comprising both political leaders and members of the KLA, the latter a splinter group of the former. Finally, the Rambouillet negotiations provide an excellent example of the impact of deadlines on proceedings. Led by Albright, the mediators in Rambouillet decided to set a specific deadline—time and date—on the negotiations in the hope that it would produce last-minute progress. It did not work, however, and the parties walked away from the table with no deal, leaving the mediators to practice Balkans shuttle diplomacy. In the end, no amount of pressure could convince Yugoslav president Milosevic to sign the agreement, triggering a full-scale international crisis.

Looking Forward

The post–cold war era presents negotiators everywhere with some new rules and new players, perhaps even a new game board. The exploration of traditional and recent trends in diplomacy has shown that many of the main parameters of negotiation have remained fairly constant through the transition (crisis, coalition building, mediation, issue linkage, and so on). So, what are the new developments in the negotiation arena? Manifestations are in evidence everywhere, from the prominence of environmental issues on the diplomatic agenda to the citizen diplomats who negotiate them in a new kind of international forum. The calculus of national interest has been greatly complicated for governments, democratic and nondemocratic alike. For the democracies of the world, diplomatic agenda setting is highly subject to strong domestic pulls; for the nondemocracies, deliberations are clearly influenced by international and public opinion. In the contemporary process, it is also clear that culture and identity play greater roles in shaping negotiation positions and moves, as manifested in the application of new techniques such as culture-based mediation and track-two facilitation.

Nonetheless, as the new century dawns, it is not possible to foresee all of the forces that will shape its international relations. The larger role now afforded nonstate entities bodes both well and ill: for all of the citizen groups now at work on health and development issues, there are also crime and drug syndicates making greater inroads. Yet, there is good reason to believe that the broadening or democratization of the diplomatic arena will continue at a rapid pace. Moreover, it is clear that technology will have a prominent role. The process of connecting people around the world to one another will undoubtedly have far-reaching implications for the diplomatic agenda and the negotiation process. The final section of this book, the afterword that immediately follows, explores the notion of virtual diplomacy, one of the newest developments on the negotiation horizon.

Afterword: Entering the World of Virtual Diplomacy

People's professional and personal lives offer them countless opportunities to refine their negotiation skills as they bargain for higher pay, cheaper products, and fairer treatment. Nevertheless, this book argues that international negotiation is a unique activity, one in which skills gained in other endeavors can be helpful but are not enough to ensure success. In the high-stakes arena of international affairs, learning on the job can be costly, even dangerous, as many of the examples have shown.

How does one gain experience and training as an international negotiator? The International Communication and Negotiation Simulations (ICONS) project at the University of Maryland has been offering a negotiation simulation activity to students since the early 1980s. The simulation places participants in the roles of diplomats for state and select nonstate actors. Working as part of a negotiation team, student participants try their hands at developing policy positions and presenting them in a *simulated* international negotiation arena. The material in the following pages describes how simulations work to enhance learning and how ICONS simulations are structured to provide students with opportunities to develop international negotiation skills. Its innovative use of the World Wide Web for research and communication purposes puts ICONS in step with some important, real-world developments in the virtual diplomacy arena.

Simulation as Active Learning in International Relations

Participation in simulations is a relatively widespread activity. Simulations or games place participants in specific roles and require that they overcome a host of obstacles in their pursuit of goals (Walcott 1980). In international relations simulations, the underlying idea is that students should walk a mile in the shoes of real-world decision makers, thus gaining insight into and appreciation for the tremendous complexities of the international system. Some of the more popular international relations exercises include the Model UN and various regional spin-offs, including the Model Organization of American States (OAS), Model Organization of African Unity (OAU), and Model NATO (Dent and Sondrol 1998). These regionally focused exercises, in which students shape policies in rapidly changing political environments, grew out of older, more theoretical exercises, such as Harold Guetzkow's Inter-Nation Simulation (Guetzkow and Cherryholmes 1966). They share with more traditional models the aim of representing decision-making environments for participants, who then attempt to navigate the complex international terrain themselves.

Simulations that focus on negotiation are also growing in popularity as more and more colleges and universities introduce courses that deal specifically with this topic. A recent edition of the journal *International Negotiation* (1998, vol. 3) provides an overview of some of these exercises, which include, in addition to ICONS, the Global Problems Summit, an issue-focused simulation. Each of these exercises—old and new, general in scope as opposed to more specific—provides students with active learning opportunities that can have lasting impact. Long after lecture notes have been lost and professors' names forgotten, few learners will forget the time they averted war for all Kenyans by forging a last-minute border agreement with neighboring Uganda!

Simulation and Virtual Diplomacy

Active learning approaches to the study of international relations and negotiation more and more reflect an important development in the *actual* international arena: the impact of new technologies on the conduct of diplomacy. Top-level diplomats who actually perform these tasks and academics who study diplomacy are increasingly gathering at workshops and conferences focused on the relevance of information technology to the relations among states. The United States Institute of Peace convened a virtual diplomacy conference in 1997 to reflect on the current role of electronic or virtual communities and the "flattening" of decision-making time in negotiations owing to the rapidity of new communication technologies (United States Institute of Peace 1997). Further speculation took place at a Fulbright International Center symposium several months later on "Foreign Policy for the Next Century." Here, distinguished presenters delivered papers with such titles as "Who Needs Embassies?" (Locke 1998).

So far, the technology is developing ahead of our understanding of its day-to-day impact. Amid all of the speculation, however, there is some evidence that states will begin to use distance technologies to reduce the need for costly outposts around the world. Langhorne (1997, 8) notes that a handful of South American countries have already begun to share diplomatic operations in Asia, augmenting their physical presence with a virtual one. For Mexico, in particular, negotiating power is devolving from the Foreign Ministry to the individual posts, whose staff now have the technologies to communicate directly with their counterparts in other countries.

ICONS offers simulation exercises that rely heavily on networked computer environments not unlike those now coming on-line in real-world diplomatic negotiations. It has long used available communication technologies to connect student negotiators with one another—even before the Internet existed in its current form. ICONS' original intent was to enhance the collaborative and cross-cultural elements of the simulated negotiations by connecting American students with peers around the United States and eventually around the world. The current confluence of interest in new technologies and diplomacy provides ICONS with a fresh opportunity to explore the relationship between communication and negotiation. Student learners stand to be the clear beneficiaries of this effort and of the many other new simulation activities that make use of Internet technology to deliver learning tools.

Among the new, technologically sophisticated simulation activities is the Generalized Decision Support System (GENIE) Project, which captures the essence of negotiation under crisis conditions. Users are confronted with choices of strategies based either on the pursuit of maximum self-gain under risky conditions or on the pursuit of mutual benefit, where more limited gains to all parties are assured. Developed by Jonathan Wilkenfeld and Sarit Kraus at the University of Maryland, GENIE uses innovative software to provide negotiators with a decision support system to aid in their decision-making process and a communications package to allow communication with their counterparts during the negotiations (Wilkenfeld et al. 1995; Santmire et al. 1998)

Using World Wide Web technology, activities in the broader diplomatic arena are simulated in the Model United Nations Security Council. Designed to bring the Model UN experience to many more students by making it available on-line, this project features video-conferencing technology to ensure replication of the face-to-face encounters so central to the actual Security Council's proceedings (Kuzma 1998). The virtual Security Council, like ICONS, is able to take advantage of the wealth of resources available via the World Wide Web, such as actual government statements and position papers, thus enhancing a student's ability to prepare for the negotiations. Both feature on-line resource libraries designed to better prepare students to play the roles they have been assigned and to access information as needed during the proceedings.

Participation in ICONS: Understanding the Process

The following information is provided for readers interested in supplement-
ing their theoretical exploration of the topic of international negotiation with
a chance to apply this negotiation knowledge—to practice the hands-on
skills that diplomats must use in their craft. Thus, this special section on
active learning and virtual diplomacy concludes with a description of the
ICONS simulation exercises. This is a tool that all three authors of this book
have worked with for many years in an effort to enhance student learning
about international relations, foreign policy, and negotiation. As described
below, ICONS gives participants the opportunity to simulate real-world
processes as governmental decision makers and international negotiators.

Getting Started

The ICONS World Wide Web site at http://www.icons.umd.edu (see
figure A.1) introduces participants to the ICONS simulation environment. The initial step in an ICONS simulation is preparation. Faculty
members first contact the ICONS staff to register their classes in the various simulation exercises that are available during the coming semester.
Each class then selects a different country to represent. The average size
for a country-team is approximately fifteen students, but it is not unusual

Figure A.1   ICONS Website: www.icons.umd.edu

to have smaller- or larger-sized groups. At the start of the semester, ICONS' staff distribute a negotiation scenario to all classes that will be participating in the simulation. (Previous and current simulation scenarios are posted on the ICONS Web site.) The scenario outlines the primary issues to be discussed—human rights, arms control, and trade, among others—and helps define the scope of the coming negotiations. Since the scenario is only a brief overview, each country-team (class of students) must conduct research on the nation whose decision makers it has chosen to portray, as well as on the issues under negotiation, so that it will be able to develop national goals and strategies for the coming negotiations.

Working Effectively in Teams

Negotiations do not simply take place among the different country-teams in each simulation, but also occur within each team as members move from the initial research phase into the policy planning stage, where goals (policies the country-team would like to see adopted) and strategies (plans for how to achieve those goals) are determined. The internal decision-making process requires that participants navigate what was described earlier in this book as the domestic-level game of the international negotiation process. Usually, teams divide themselves into subgroups according to the different negotiation areas outlined in the scenario document that launches the simulation. However, this initial assignment of tasks often leads to competing interests and internal disputes within the team (as, for example, when human rights and security specialists are concerned with achieving different, possibly conflicting, goals). Each team will have to determine ways to resolve these disputes and work together effectively, so that it can bring coherent policies to the negotiation table. Each team's creation of a jointly developed position paper or negotiation brief encourages this collaboration; this document will serve as an internal working paper to guide the team in the negotiation process. (A sample position paper outline is also available on the ICONS Web site.)

Negotiating with International Counterparts

The next step in the ICONS process is the on-line negotiation component. On a specified date, the country-team begins an on-line dialogue with the other country-teams and whichever nonstate actors are represented in the negotiations. The negotiation phase of the simulation process normally lasts from three to five weeks, with about twenty country-teams participating. Teams start by logging on to the negotiation community and sending initial policy statements on every negotiation issue to their counterparts. The simulation itself really begins as the country-teams start responding to each others' statements with questions, suggestions, clarifications, and requests. As the simulation continues, it is important to keep in mind that, as in the real world, the negotiators themselves determine the course and the outcome of these negotiations.

Developing a Strategy

Strategy is an important consideration during the negotiation phase, as each team concerns itself with trying to make progress on the critical issues before it, while at the same time trying to protect its own national interests. Balancing these two tasks takes work and requires that participants carefully consider the messages they receive from their counterparts, as well as convey their own positions clearly and convincingly. As discussed earlier in the book, creating a collaborative or problem-solving negotiation environment takes work. If a country-team strives only to achieve its own national goals, it is unlikely that others will meet it halfway. Inevitably, some concessions must be made to facilitate progress.

Sending Communiqués

Participants in ICONS negotiations communicate in two ways; these are intended to mirror the kinds of interactions that negotiators have with each other in the real world. The first involves sending statements or communiqués. In general, these messages convey positions on the various issues under negotiation and respond to the communications received from the other country-teams. (See figure A.2 for a sample communiqué.) These

Figure A.2 Sample Communiqué

Message # 765	From: Russia	Apr 10, 1998 03:38

To: France,Russia,Simcon.

Issues: Debt/Development

Subject: NOGDA - 2

Greetings France.

Russia would like to add to the earlier request for more specific information.
1. The biggest difficulty we see with NOGDA is the question of how NOGDA will avoid becoming imperialist--as Asian countries presently view the IMF?
2. What will stop corporations, NGOs (not known for their economic prosperity), and others from becoming as powerful as the first world countries represented by the IMF are?
3. What will prevent the "economic experts" employed by NOGDA from becoming economic power lords who direct the fate of developing countries?
4. All actors who donate will be members in NOGDA; are *receiving* actors members too?
5. How will NOGDA alleviate debt and dependency cycles? Simply by facilitating aid to those countries in need? Or by the requirement to reform banking policies before aid is granted?

With thanks and respect, Russia encourages further explanation of your proposal.

Read New Messages	Search Archives	Send Message	Administrative
Enter Conference	Search Conference Archives		Exit Community

communiqués can be sent at any time of the day or night, and are posted to the negotiation community to be picked up when the recipient signs on to the system. Because collaboration is much more realistic than individually crafted negotiation policies, the issue specialists on a team should try, whenever possible, to construct statements jointly and work out policy responses together. Of course, this can often be difficult, given busy schedules, but it is important that the team as a whole and the issue subgroups develop procedures to ensure that the negotiations are truly a group effort.

Participating in Real-Time Conferences

The second kind of communication that occurs during the negotiations is the real-time conference. Several conferences are held during the three-to-five-week duration of the on-line negotiations, and each focuses on one of the negotiation issues. The conference is guided by an agenda, which outlines any important proposals and other matters under consideration. Representatives from each team assemble at a predetermined time (for example, 1400 Greenwich Mean Time on February 14) and begin to work through the items on this agenda. A simulation coordinator (SIMCON) from ICONS, a staffer who monitors the exercise on a daily basis, acts as the chairperson for this real-time conversation. The conferences are especially exciting because teams know they will be engaged in an on-line negotiation with peers from around the world. Moreover, the conferences allow all country-teams to respond to each other immediately, and give the negotiators a concentrated time in which to work to reach agreements—or at least to determine what obstacles are keeping them from making progress.

Assessing Outcomes

Since ICONS simulations are short in duration, they can really only provide a snapshot of the negotiation process. Participants can sometimes be frustrated by the lack of apparent progress in the negotiations as they come to a close. They must be reminded that a simulation is not meant to replicate the entire negotiation process. To do this faithfully, the negotiations would have to run for months or even years! Instead, the intention is that participants will learn firsthand about the many complexities decision makers face in the negotiation arena. The best way to determine whether a simulation was successful is not to look for specific outcomes, but to look at what progress was made in negotiating each of the issues. During the debriefing phase, each country-team facilitator (the classroom instructor) will usually ask the group to reflect on what was accomplished during the course of the negotiations, including frustrations with the process. (Sample debriefing questions are available on the ICONS Web site.) During this time, SIMCON also provides summary comments on team performance during the negotiations. The simulation participants themselves, however, are the best judges of what was actually accomplished.

References

AbiNader, Jean. 1998. "The Gulf between the Arabs and America." *Washington Post*, 1 March: C1, C5.

Ahrari, M. E., and Brigid Starkey. 1997. "Polarity and Stability in the Post-Cold War Persian Gulf." *The Fletcher Forum of World Affairs* 21, no. 1 (Winter/Spring): 133–151.

Alliance of Small Island States. 1997. "A NGO Perspective on the United Nations Barbados Plan of Action for Small Island Developing States." 10–14 November. <http://www.aosis.org/meeting.htm>

Anderson, Dean. 1995. "Rapporteur's Report of Workshop Presentations and Discussions." In *The Emerging International Regime for Climate Change: Structures and Options after Berlin,* ed. Michael Grubb and Dean Anderson. London: Royal Institute of International Affairs: 7–44.

Associated Press and Reuters. 1998. "Russia PM Plays Down Loan Hopes at IMF Talks." *CNN Interactive.* 2 December. <http://cnn.com/WORLD/europe/9812/02/russia.imf.01/ index.html>

Axelrod, Robert M. 1984. *The Evolution of Cooperation.* New York: Basic Books.

Axelrod, Robert M., and Robert Keohane. 1986. "Achieving Cooperation under Anarchy: Strategies and Institutions." In *Cooperation under Anarchy,* ed. Kenneth E. Oye. Princeton, N.J.: Princeton University Press: 226–254.

Barber, Benjamin R. 1995. *Jihad vs. McWorld: How Globalism and Tribalism Are Reshaping the World.* New York: Ballantine Books.

Barr, Cameron, and Lawrence J. Goodrich. 1997. "The Future of the Kyoto Climate Accord Is Still Up in the Air." *Christian Science Monitor International.* 12 December. <http://www.csmonitor.com/durable/1997/12/12/intl/intl.6.html>

BBC News. 1997. "Agreement at Kyoto Climate Conference." 10 December. <http://news2.thdo.bbc.co.uk/hi/english/despatches/newsid%5F380 00/38374.stm>

Bercovitch, Jacob. 1997. "Mediation in International Conflict: An Overview of Theory, a Review of Practice." In *Peacemaking in International Conflict: Methods and Techniques,* ed. I. William Zartman and J. Lewis Rasmussen. Washington, D.C.: U.S. Institute for Peace Press: 125–153.

Bernstein, Thomas. 1995. "Muted Differences: The Negotiations to Normalize U.S.-Chinese Relations." Institute for the Study of Diplomacy, Case Number 426. *Pew Case Studies in International Affairs.*Washington, D.C.: Georgetown University.

Bobrow, Davis B. 1981. "The Perspective of Great Power Foreign Policy." In *Dynamics of Third Party Intervention: Kissinger and the Middle East*, ed. Jeffrey Z. Rubin. New York: Praeger: 171–196.

Boyer, Mark A. 1999a. "Clubs, Polities, and Overlapping Collectivities: Understanding the Potential for Cooperation in a Post-Hegemonic World." In *New Frontiers in International Relations Theory*, ed. Yale Ferguson and R. J. Barry Jones. Albany: SUNY Press.

_____. 1999b. "Issue Definition and Two-Level Games: An Application to the American Foreign Policy Process." *Diplomacy and Statecraft* (November): in press.

Brams, Steven J., and Jeffrey M. Togman. 1998. "Cooperation through Threats: The Northern Ireland Case." *PS: Political Science and Politics* 31, no. 1 (March): 32–39.

Brecher, Michael, and Jonathan Wilkenfeld. 1997. *A Study of Crisis*. Ann Arbor: University of Michigan Press.

Buck, Lori, Nicole Gallant, and Kim Richard Nossal. 1998. "Sanctions as a Gendered Instrument of Statecraft." *Review of International Studies* 24, no. 1 (January): 69–84.

Carter, Jimmy. 1982. *Keeping Faith: Memoirs of a President*. New York: Bantam Books.

CNN Interactive. 1997. "Global Warming Pact Fuels U.S. Debate." 14 December. <http://cnn.com/EARTH/9712/14/climate.treaty/index.html>

Cohen, Eliot A. 1997. "Military Power and International Order." In *Managing Global Chaos: Sources of and Responses to International Conflict*, ed. Chester Crocker, Fen Osler Hampson, and Pamela Aall. Washington, D.C.: United States Institute of Peace Press: 223–236.

Cohen, Raymond. 1997. *Negotiating across Cultures*, 2nd ed. Washington, D.C.: United States Institute of Peace Press.

Colosi, Thomas R. 1986. "The Iceberg Principle: Secrecy in Negotiation." In *Perspectives on Negotiation: Four Case Studies and Interpretations*, ed. Diane B. Bendahmane and John W. McDonald, Jr. Washington, D.C.: Center for the Study of Foreign Affairs.

Conybeare, John. 1986. "Trade Wars: A Comparative Study of Anglo-Hanse, Franco-Italian, and Smoot-Hawley Conflicts." In *Cooperation under Anarchy*, ed. Kenneth E. Oye. Princeton, N.J.: Princeton University Press: 147–172.

Cooper, Richard N. 1998. "Toward a Real Global Warming Treaty." *Foreign Affairs* 77, no. 2 (March/April): 66–79.

Dent, David W., and Paul Sondrol. 1998. "Teaching through Simulation: The Model OAS." *LASA Forum* 27, no. 4 (Winter): 8–14.

Dixit, Avinash K., and Barry Nalebuff. 1991. *Thinking Strategically: The Competitive Edge in Business, Politics, and Everyday Life*. New York: W. W. Norton.

Donahue, Thomas R. 1991. "The Case against NAFTA." *Columbia Journal of World Business* 26: 91–95.

Downs, George W., David M. Rocke, and Randolph M. Siverson. 1986. "Arms Race and Cooperation." In *Cooperation under Anarchy*, ed. Kenneth E. Oye. Princeton, N.J.: Princeton University Press: 118–146.

Driscoll, David D. 1997. "What Is the International Monetary Fund?" July. <http://www.imf.org/external/pubs/ft/exrp/what.htm>

Druckman, Daniel, and Benjamin Broome. 1991. "Value Differences and Conflict Resolution: Familiarity or Liking?" *Journal of Conflict Resolution* 35, no. 4 (December): 571–593.

Environmental News Network. 1997. "Kyoto Pact Reached, No Promise of Ratification." 11 December. <http://www.enn.com/specialreports/climate/news/kyotoends.asp>

Fedarko, Kevin. 1993. "Swimming the Oslo Channel." *Time.* September: 50–51.

Ferguson, Yale H., and Richard W. Mansbach. 1996. "The Past as Prelude to the Future? Identities and Loyalties in Global Politics." In *Culture and Identity in IR Theory*, ed.Yosef Lapid and Friedrich Kratochwil. Boulder, Colo.: Lynne Rienner Publishers: 21–44.

Fisher, Roger, and William Ury. 1991. *Getting to Yes: Negotiating Agreements without Giving In*, 2nd ed. New York: Penguin.

Fisher, Roger, et al. 1997. *Coping with International Conflict.* Upper Saddle River, N.J.: Prentice-Hall.

Freeman, Chas. W., Jr. 1997a. *Arts of Power: Statecraft and Diplomacy.* Washington, D.C.: United States Institute of Peace Press.

_____. 1997b. *The Diplomat's Dictionary.* Rev. ed. Washington, D.C.: United States Institute of Peace Press.

George, Alexander L. 1997. *Forceful Persuasion: Coercive Diplomacy as an Alternative to War.* Washington, D.C.: United States Institute of Peace.

Guetzkow, Harold, and Cleo H. Cherryholmes. 1966. *Inter-Nation Simulation Kit.* Chicago: Science Research Associates.

Haas, Peter M. 1992. "Introduction: Epistemic Communities and International Policy Coordination." *International Organization* 46, no. 1 (Winter): 1–36.

Haass, Richard N. 1997. "Using Force: Lessons and Choices for U.S. Foreign Policy." In *Managing Global Chaos: Sources of and Responses to International Conflict*, ed. Chester Crocker, Fen Osler Hampson, and Pamela Aall. Washington, D.C.: United States Institute of Peace Press: 197–208.

Hardin, Garrett. 1968. "The Tragedy of the Commons." *Science* 162 (13 December): 1243–1248.

Harrigan, Steve, Associated Press, and Reuters. 1998. "IMF Lauds Russian Recovery Plan but Withholds More Aid." *CNN Interactive.* 2 December. <http://cnn.com/WORLD/europe/9812/02/russia.imf.02/>

Hartford *Courant.* 1991. "Is CNN Being Used for Iraqi Propaganda?" 21 January: A6.

Hook, Steven W. 1995. *National Interest and Foreign Aid.* Boulder, Colo.: Lynne Rienner Publishers.

Hopmann, P. Terrence. 1996. *The Negotiation Process and the Resolution of International Conflicts.* Columbia, S.C.: University of South Carolina Press.

Houghton, John T., G. J. Jenkins, and J. J. Ephraums. 1990. *Climate Change: The IPCC Scientific Assessment 1990.* Cambridge: Cambridge University Press.

Huntington, Samuel P. 1993. "The Clash of Civilizations?" *Foreign Affairs* 73, no. 3 (Summer): 22–49.

Ingraham, Jesson. 1999. "The Irish Peace Process." 2 February. <http://cain.ulst.ac.uk/events/peace/talks.htm.>

Jarman, Neil. 1997. *Material Conflicts: Parades and Visual Displays in Northern Ireland*. Oxford, U.K.: Berg Publishers.

Jeffrey, Charles, ed. 1997. *The Regional Dimension of the European Union*. London: Frank Cass Publishers.

Kaufman, Joyce P. 1998a. "The Teaching of International Negotiation—Editor's Introduction." *International Negotiation* (Special Edition) 3: 1–5.

_____. 1998b. "Using Simulation as a Tool to Teach about International Negotiation." *International Negotiation* (Special Edition) 3: 59–75.

Kennan, George. 1997. "Diplomacy without Diplomats?" *Foreign Affairs* 76, no. 5 (September/October): 198–212.

Kennedy, Robert F. 1969. *The Thirteen Days: A Memoir of the Cuban Missile Crisis*. New York: W. W. Norton and Co.

Kerrigan, Karen. 1997. "Viewpoint: Global Warming Treaty Damages U.S." *Business News*. 27 October. <http://www.amcity.com/dayton/stories/102797/editorial4.html>

Kratochwil, Friedrich. 1984. "Thrasymmachos Revisited: On the Relevance of Norms and the Study of Law for International Relations." *Journal of International Affairs* 37, no. 2 (Winter): 343–356.

Kuzma, Lynn M. 1998. "The World Wide Web and Active Learning in the International Relations Classroom." *PS: Political Science and Politics* 31, no. 3 (September): 578–584.

Langhorne, Richard. 1997. "Current Developments in Diplomacy: Who Are the Diplomats Now?" *Diplomacy and Statecraft* 8, no. 2 (July): 1–15.

Lewis, Richard D. 1996. *When Cultures Collide: Managing Successfully across Cultures*. Sonoma, Calif.: Nicholas Brealy Publishing.

Locke, Mary. 1998. "Who Needs Embassies?" Paper presented at Foreign Policy for the Next Century conference, 2 June, Washington, D.C.: Academy for International Development.

Lumsdaine, David H. 1993. *Moral Vision in International Politics: The Foreign Aid Regime, 1949–1989*. Princeton, N.J.: Princeton University Press.

Mansbach, Richard. 1997. *The Global Puzzle*, 2nd. ed. New York: Houghton-Mifflin.

Matthews, Jessica. 1997. "Power Shift." *Foreign Affairs* 76, no. 1 (January/February): 50–67.

Media Reality Check. 1997. "Media Research Center Cyberalert: Full Gore on Kyoto." 15 December. <http://www.mrc.org/news/cyberalert/1997/cyb19971215.html>

Mo, Jongryn. 1994. "The Logic of Two-Level Games with Endogenous Domestic Coalitions." *Journal of Conflict Resolution* 38, no. 3: 402–422.

_____. 1995. "Domestic Institutions and International Bargaining: The Role of Agent Veto in Two-Level Games." *American Political Science Review* 89, no. 4: 914–924.

Moore, Thomas Gale. 1998. *Climate of Fear: Why We Shouldn't Worry about Global Warming*. Washington, D.C.: CATO Institute.

Mott, Richard N. 1997. "Can Gore's Actions Match His Lofty Words?" *Japan Times Online*. 5 December. <http://www.japantimes.co.jp/cop3/indepth/mott.html>

Murray, John S. 1986. "Understanding Competing Theories of Negotiation." *Negotiation Journal* 2, no. 2 (April): 179–186.

Mushakoji, Kinhide. 1976. "The Cultural Premises of Japanese Diplomacy." In *The Silent Power: Japan's Identity and World Role,* ed. Japan Center for International Exchange. Tokyo: Simul Press: 35–49.

Nelan, Bruce W. 1998. "Can This Deal Work?" *TIME.com.* 9 March. <http://cgi.pathfinder.com/time/magazine/1998/dom/980309/world.can_this_deal_work29.html>

Official Documentation and Information from Norway. *Ministry of Fisheries Homepage.* <http://odin.dep.no/fid/eng/>

Oka, Takashi. 1992. "Tools for a U.S.–Japan Partnership." *Christian Science Monitor,* 27 November: 18A.

Oye, Kenneth E., ed. 1986. *Cooperation under Anarchy.* Princeton, N.J.: Princeton University Press.

Peterson, V. Spike, and Anne Sisson Runyan. 1993. *Global Gender Issues.* Boulder, Colo.: Westview Press.

Ponce, Mercedes M., ed. 1997. "The Florida Connection: Florida's Position on the Free Trade Area of the Americas." May. <http://americas.fiu.edu/americas/americas-frames-noblue.html>

Princen, Thomas. 1992. *Intermediaries in International Conflict.* Princeton, N.J.: Princeton University Press.

Putnam, Robert D. 1988. "Diplomacy and Domestic Politics: The Logic of Two-Level Games." *International Organization* 42, no. 3: 427–460.

Raiffa, Howard. 1982. *The Art and Science of Negotiation.* Cambridge: Harvard University Press.

Rasmussen, J. Lewis. 1997. "Peacemaking in the Twenty-First Century: New Rules, New Roles, New Actors." In *Peacemaking in International Conflict: Methods and Techniques,* ed. I. William Zartman and J. Lewis Rasmussen. Washington, D.C.: United States Institute of Peace Press: 23–50.

Raum, Tom. 1998. "House Refuses to Consider Clinton's $18 Billion IMF Package." *CNN Interactive.* 17 September. <http://cnn.com/ALLPOLITICS/stories/1998/09/17/imf.package/>

Reno, William. 1996. "Business Conflict and the Shadow State: The Case of West Africa." In *Business and the State in International Relations,* ed. Ronald W. Cox. Boulder, Colo.: Westview Press: 149–163.

Reuters and Associated Press. 1995. "Peace Will Lead to Palestinian State within 2 Years, Says Arafat." 25 October. <http://www.detnews.com/menu/stories/21693.htm>

Robinson, Gillian. 1992. "Cross-Community Marriage in Northern Ireland." <http://www.qub.ac.uk/ss/csr/index.html>

Rosenfeld, Stephen S. 1998. "Kofi Annan's Reminder." *Washington Post,* 27 February: A25.

Rourke, John T., Ralph G. Carter, and Mark A. Boyer. 1996. *Making American Foreign Policy,* 2nd ed. Guilford, Conn.: Brown and Benchmark.

Ruggie, John G. 1975. "International Responses to Technology: Concepts and Trends." *International Organization* 29 (Summer): 552–584.

Sandler, Todd. 1997. *Global Challenges.* Cambridge, U.K.: Cambridge University Press.

Santmire, Tara, et al. 1998. "Differences in Cognitive Complexity Levels among Negotiators and Crisis Outcomes." *Political Psychology* 19, no. 4. (December): 721–748.

Schmemann, Serge, and Steven Erlanger. 1998. "Mideast Marathon: How 9 Days of Talks Ended in 'The Long Night.'" *Washington Post*, 25 October: A1, A14.

Sebenius, James. 1984. *Negotiating the Law of the Sea*. Cambridge: Harvard University Press.

Shenon, Philip. 1998. "America Takes On a Struggle with Domestic Costs." *New York Times*, 23 August: sect. 4, p. 1.

Sick, Gary. 1985. *All Fall Down: America's Fateful Encounter with Iran*. London: I. B. Taurus.

Skocpol, Theda. 1988. "The Limits of the New Deal System and the Roots of Contemporary Welfare Dilemmas." In *The Politics of Policy in the United States*, ed. Margaret Weir, Ann Shola Orloft, and Theda Skocpol. Princeton, N.J.: Princeton University Press: 293–311.

Smith, Fred, and Jim Sheehan. 1997. "Kyoto Gets Gored." *CEI Update*. 8 December. <http://www.junkscience.com/news/kyoto6.htm>

Smith, R. Jeffrey. 1998. "Document Indicates Illicit Russia-Iraq Deal." *Washington Post.Com*. 12 February. <http://washingtonpost.com/wp-srv/inatl/longterm/iraq/stories/iraq021298.htm>

Snyder, Glenn, and Paul Deising. 1977. *Conflict among Nations*. Princeton, N.J.: Princeton University Press.

Spero, Joan Edelman. 1990. *The Politics of International Economic Relations*, 4th ed. New York: St. Martin's Press.

Starkey, Brigid. 1994. "Negotiation Training through Simulation: The ICONS International Negotiation Seminars." *Educator's Tech Exchange* (Spring): 6–11.

Starkey, Brigid, and Jonathan Wilkenfeld. 1996. "Project ICONS: Computer-Assisted Negotiations for the IR Classroom." *International Studies Notes* 21, no. 1 (Winter): 25–29.

Taylor, Philip. 1984. *Nonstate Actors in International Politics: From Transregional to Substate Organizations*. Boulder, Colo.: Westview Press.

Torney-Purta, Judith. 1998. "Evaluating Programs Designed to Teach International Content and Negotiation Skills." *International Negotiation* (Special Edition) 3: 77–97.

Trumbore, Peter F., and Mark A. Boyer. 1998. "Two-Level Negotiations in International Crisis: Testing the Impact of Regime Type and Issue Area." Unpublished manuscript, University of Connecticut.

United Nations. 1998. "Letter from the Executive Chairman of the Special Commission to the President of the Security Council." 22 January. <http://www.un.org/Depts/unscom/s98-58.htm>

United Nations Environment Programme. "Information Unit for Conventions (IUC)." <http://www.cop3.de/fccc/climate/fact23.htm>

United Nations Framework Convention on Climate Change. <http://www.unfccc.de/>

U.S. Department of State. 1998. "Remarks at Town Hall Meeting, Ohio State University. Columbus, Ohio, 18 February 1998." Transcript released by the Office of the Spokesman. 20 February.

United States Institute of Peace. 1997. *Virtual Diplomacy Conference*. 2 April, Washington, D.C.

Walcott, Charles, ed. 1980. *Simple Simulations II*. Washington, D.C.: American Political Science Association.

Warrick, Joby. 1997. "Climate Pact Rescued in Final Hours." *Washington Post*, 13 December: A1.

Washington Post. 1998. "Iraq: Road to the Current Crisis." 15 February: A34.

Wilkenfeld, Jonathan. 1991. "Trigger-Response Transitions in Foreign Policy Crises, 1929–1985." *Journal of Conflict Resolution* 35, no. 1 (March): 143–169.

Wilkenfeld, Jonathan, and Joyce Kaufman. 1993. "Political Science: Network Simulation in International Politics." *Social Science Computer Review* 11, no. 4 (Winter): 464–476.

Wilkenfeld, Jonathan, et al. 1995. "GENIE: A Decision Support System for Crisis Negotiation." *Decision Support Systems* 14: 369–391.

Young, Oran. 1968. *The Politics of Force: Bargaining during International Crises*. Princeton, N.J.: Princeton University Press.

Zang, Malina Poshtova. 1998. "Russian Bears Trample Dow." CNN Financial Network Online. 26 August. <http://cnnfn.com/markets/9808/26/marketopen/>

Zartman, I. William, and Maureen Berman. 1982. *The Practical Negotiator*. New Haven, Conn.: Yale University Press.

Zartman, I. William, and Saadia Touval. 1996. "International Mediation in the Post-Cold War Era." In *Managing Global Chaos: Sources of and Responses to International Conflict*, ed. Chester Crocker, Fen Osler Hampson, and Pamela Aall. Washington, D.C.: United States Institute of Peace Press: 445–461.

Zimmerman, William. 1973. "Issue Area and Foreign Policy Process: A Research Note in Search of a General Theory." *American Political Science Review* 67: 1204–1212.

Index

action-reaction process (in negotiations). *See* sequential games

actor (negotiator) characteristics: actors, number of, 35–36; coalitions, number of, 35–36; commitment, 40–41, 82–83; power distribution, 37–38; team models, 36–37. *See also* negotiators

adversarial diplomacy, 112

agreements (in negotiation), 46–47

Albright, Madeleine (U.S. Secretary of State): and Iraqi crisis, 18, 20, 23, 84

Allied Coalition against Iraq, 17, 18, 19, 27–28; criticism of, 17

Annan, Kofi (UN Secretary General): mission to Iraq, 7, 17, 20, 21, 23–25

Arab-Israeli conflicts: and polarity impact, 30; web sites, 50–51. *See also* Camp David Accord; Oslo Accords

arms races, 101

Aziz, Tariq (Deputy Prime Minister, Iraq), 18, 20, 21, 23, 24

balance of power, 28–30

bargaining. *See* negotiations

Berlin Mandate (on emissions control), 9, 10. *See also* Climate Change Conference

bipolarity, 29, 30, 35; and Arab-Israeli negotiations, 30

Bosnia conflict: and mediation, 120; and track-two diplomacy, 124

Bush, George (U.S. president): diplomatic style, 82; and Iraqi crisis, 17, 19; and NAFTA, 81

Butler, Richard (UNSCOM director), 18, 20, 24

Camp David Accord (1978), 57; and interest-based bargaining, 115

Carter, James (U.S. president), 57

case analysis. *See* Kosovo peace negotiations

chicken (game model), 98–100, 107–108; and Cuban Missile Crisis, 100; and international crisis, 100. *See also* simultaneous games

chief of government model (in negotiations), 91–92

Chirac, Jacques (president, France), 20–21, 23

Climate Change Conference, Kyoto (1997), 6, 7, 8–16, 75, 80, 81, 85; agreements, 15–16; background, 8–9; compromise, 15–16; and governments, 10–11; and Iraq arms inspections crisis, comparison to 6–8; issues of, 12–14, 81–82; negotiation strategies, 14–16; and nongovernmental groups, 11–12; participants, 10–12; setup, 9–10; and the United States, 10–16; web sites, 25–26, 73

Clinton, William (U.S. president), 18, 20, 22, 85–86, 118–120; and NAFTA, 81; and Northern Ireland, 86

Coalition of Member States Cooperating with Kuwait. *See* Allied Coalition against Iraq

145

Index

About the Authors

Dr. Brigid Starkey is associate director of the International Communication and Negotiation Simulations (ICONS) Project at the University of
Maryland, College Park. She teaches an introductory level course on
international negotiation, using the ICONS simulation and a case study
approach. She publishes in the area of interactive learning for the college
classroom and on conflict and security in the Middle East. Her publica-
tions include "Using Computers to Connect across Cultural Divides" in
Education, Technology, Power: Educational Computing as Social Practice,
edited by H. Bromley and M. Apple (SUNY Press, 1998) and "Polarity
and Stability in the Post-Cold War Persian Gulf" with M. E. Ahari in *The
Fletcher Forum of World Affairs* (1997).

Dr. Mark Boyer is an associate professor of political science at the University of Connecticut and director of the Connecticut Project in International Negotiation (CPIN). He was Pew Faculty Fellow in International
Affairs and an SSRC-MacArthur Fellow in International Peace and Security. He is the author of *International Cooperation and Public Goods* (Johns
Hopkins, 1993) and co-author (with John Rourke) of *World Politics*, 2nd
ed. (McGraw-Hill, 1998), among others. He has published in the *Journal
of Conflict Resolution, Review of International Political Economy, International
Journal, Social Science Computer Review, Defence Economics*, and *Diplomacy
and Statecraft*.

Dr. Jonathan Wilkenfeld is professor and chair of the Department of Government and Politics at the University of Maryland, College Park. He is
also the founder and executive director of the International Communication and Negotiation Simulations (ICONS) Project. He has published
widely in the area of foreign policy analysis, international crisis, negotiation, and simulation. His most recent book, *A Study of Crisis*, was co-
authored with Michael Brecher (University of Michigan Press, 1997).